EVERY
BOY'S
DREAM

EVERY

ENGLAND'S FOOTBALL FUTURE ON THE LINE

BOY'S

CHRIS GREEN

DREAM

BLOOMSBURY

LONDON · NEW DELHI · NEW YORK · SYDNEY

First published in 2009, reprinted 2012
A&C Black Publishers Ltd, an imprint of Bloomsbury Publishing Plc.
50 Bedford Square, London WC1B 3DP
www.bloomsbury.com

ISBN 978-1-4081-1216-8

10 9 8 7 6 5 4 3

A CIP catalogue record for this book is available from the British Library.

Acknowledgements
Cover photograph © Corbis
Designed by James Watson

Typeset in Sabon by seagulls.net

Printed and bound in Great Britain by CPI Group (UK) Ltd, Croydon CR0 4YY

CONTENTS

ACKNOWLEDGEMENTS

This book is the result of many years' worth of research into the subject of youth development.

It would not have been possible without the immense amount of information I have gathered over the years – including conversations with people at all levels of sport, politics and education.

Particular thanks should go to everyone I have interviewed in the fresh research for this book including Mike Foster and Tim Vine at the Premier League; John Nagle for lining up a holy trinity of Football League interviewees, Michael Tattersall, Graham Hawkins and Jim Briden; and Alan Sykes at League Football Education.

Special thanks too should go to Sir Trevor Brooking at the FA and Howard Wilkinson of the League Managers Association, who have both spoken to me many times about this subject.

I would also like to thank the Secretary of State for Culture, Media and Sport, Andy Burnham, for sparing the time in his busy ministerial schedule to discuss the issues raised in this book.

Thanks to all the boys and parents who have opened their doors and sometimes their hearts and without whose true life stories I could not have written this book or had the inspiration to ask awkward questions to people in authority.

I owe a distinct debt of gratitude to Paul Cooper, Rick Fenoglio and Andy Pitchford for opening my eyes to a fresh aspect of the beautiful game, the philosophy of Give Us Back Our Game, and to Bob Marley and Andy Barnett of the Midland Junior Premier Football League, who have shown enormous dedication to developing a youth league benefiting thousands of boys.

This book would not have been possible without the views of people actually working in youth development at professional clubs – in particular Tony Whelan at Manchester United, Aston Villa academy director Brian Jones and education and welfare officer Paul Brackwell, Dave Parnaby at Middlesbrough, Huw Jennings at Fulham FC, Tim Ball, Ian Smithson and Tim Cox at Watford FC's Academy, and Tony Daws and Guy Parkin at Scunthorpe United.

I would also like to thank former teenage footballers Ricky Clarke and Jason Blunt for their honest tales, and the many educationalists interviewed – especially Dave Woollaston of the English Schools FA, Nigel Robbins at Cirencester College, Glyn Harding at the University of Worcester, Jamie Bennett at Sports Ed and Steve Underwood of South London Schools FA.

Some people went beyond merely offering their opinions. Bert-Jan Heijmans, the Dutch coach at Brandon FC, made sure I was well fed and watered (or wined!) during our kitchen table conversations.

There have also been BBC colleagues who commissioned programmes and features about differing aspects of youth development that allowed me to develop an acute understanding of the subject – in particular Ian Bent as editor of BBC Radio 5's *On the Line*, and Jonathan Wall, former editor at *Sport on Five*.

My good friend and colleague David Conn, arguably the most astute writer on the football business in the country for the *Guardian*, also deserves thanks for the advice he has offered down the years.

From past interviews I would like to thank the likes of Dario Gradi, Richard Hodgson, Dave Richardson, John Bilton, Chris Evans, John Fry, John Baldwin, Steve Boocock, Andy Beaglehole, John Morton and the late Dave Bullas.

Thanks to my literary agent Robert Dudley and commissioning editor at A&C Black, Charlotte Atyeo.

Finally, I want to express my eternal gratitude to the two most important people in my life – my wife, Teresa, and our gorgeous son, Nicholas.

Mere words are really not enough to describe the support I've had from Teresa, who aside from being the fastest sub editor in the West (Midlands!) has offered her customary love, support and ... tolerance.

Finally, thanks and patience for one so young must go to Nicholas who has brought more joy to our lives than he will ever know.

Nicholas has just started playing football, so I will have to put into practice the perils of becoming a pushy parent outlined in this book. I have, however, no desire to live my dreams through him – just having such a warm-hearted son is enough.

When I read the manuscript of this book it quickly brought home all the varied frustrations felt by the different sectors of our national sport, football. It has given numerous people involved in different stages of football development their opportunity to pinpoint where perhaps mistakes are being made, and quite rightly highlighted where excellent programmes of good practice are being produced. There is certainly no lack of knowledge in England about how good coaches and players should be supported, but clearly there is a vacuum in leadership, which could make so many hopeful aspirations into a rewarding reality.

Much of the book focuses on the player pathway into the elite game, and those childhood dreams that may take an enthusiastic youngster from a kick-about in their back garden, through to centre stage at Wembley in front of 90,000 fans. For over 99 per cent of our young generation those dreams are never fulfilled but hopefully, despite that, they will still retain their love of the game and stay within football as either a player, coach, fan or volunteer at grassroots level. I have never really believed in separating grassroots player pathways from those in the elite game because they surely must overlap each other if the game of football continues to flourish in popularity.

Although I am quoted in the book as a Football Association staff member, my comments in this particular foreword are purely as someone who has been lucky enough to enjoy a lifetime within the game. No one person has all the answers because each generation cycle is different and the modern game changes more quickly now than ever before.

What I believe we must all accept is that for a country of some 60 million people we are not producing the depth of players at the top level with the necessary technical skills now required by the major club and international teams.

If we want to increase the number of English players competing at the highest level, then radical change is needed. This statement is nothing new because Howard Wilkinson's *FA Charter of Quality* published in 1997 was introduced as a direct result of similar concerns expressed back then. Everyone acknowledged this was a significant move in the right direction, but the natural assumption was that it would continually be updated to reflect the obvious improvements necessary as the programme evolved. Unfortunately such progress has been somewhat neutralised as gradually in recent years the two professional leagues have assumed authority and the regulation of clubs within their own structures.

In the summer of 2006 FA staff suggested an Elite Coaching Working Group, with Academy Directors and Centre of Excellence Coaches all sharing examples of good practice, which would revamp the *Charter for Quality*. The three Chief Executives from The FA, Premier League and Football League were not convinced by this proposal and instead commissioned Richard Lewis, from Rugby Football League, to conduct his own *Review into Young Player Development in Professional Football*, published a year later in the summer of 2007, with over sixty credible recommendations to take the game forward. Lewis also clearly stated that any realistic success would only happen if any emerging group appointed to lead this work would include representatives who had a technical football background. Sadly, this key issue was never implemented, and although a Youth Development Group, chaired by Howard Wilkinson, was set up in the spring of 2008, it was subsequently disbanded early in 2009 without ever being able to get beyond an agreement on the Terms of Reference.

A coordinated coaching structure and philosophy is still desperately needed, with significant investment and resources to support all of the different staff at the professional clubs. I have always wanted the FA, as the governing body, to lead this strategic role, as every federation does in all other UEFA countries. England must ensure a long-term plan, funded accordingly, that enables both elite and grassroots coaches to interact more closely than is currently the case. The games programmes, age-appropriate courses, travel time, registered numbers of players and even greater emphasis on development time are just a few of the required changes. Club priorities are naturally far more short-term focused and that is why *Every Boy's Dream* must be preserved for the future.

CHAPTER 1

ENGLAND EXPECTS

English football has had very few zeitgeist moments. One of the most appealing things about the game is its sheer relentless continuum – the constant grind through wind and rain, week in, week out – the pain, the glory, the sheer bloody-mindedness of it all.

It is hard to detect any moments of real significance before the Second World War – maybe because footy-wise, we still thought we ruled the waves. We didn't care much for the World Cup or had particularly strong views on what 'the world' had done with the game we'd created. Not as long as our local clubs won ... or lost.

The most moving moments have been in the past 50 years or so. These were mainly disasters, such as the Munich air crash in 1958 which claimed the lives of eight members of the Busby Babes, and the deaths of fans at Bolton, Ibrox and, in the 1980s, Heysel, Bradford and Hillsborough, which changed the nature of British stadiums forever.

Those dark days have been punctuated by chinks of light – England's joy at lifting the World Cup at Wembley in 1966 (for Scots it would probably be defeating the newly crowned World Champions at the same ground less than a year later), Sir Matt Busby's rebuilt team lifting the European Cup ten years after Munich and plucky performances by the national team at Italia 90 and Euro 96 when England were arguably the best team in the tournament.

The remaining moments of note include several kicks-up-the-backside. Hungary's 'Magnificent Magyars' gave the England national team a football masterclass at Wembley in 1953 with a 6-3 hammering – the first defeat to a non-British nation on home soil. In the 1970s there was a collective squirm at England failing to reach the World Cups of 1974 and 1978. Maradona's 'Hand of God' goal at the 1986 World Cup finals was controversial and memorable but hardly a defining moment for English football. Likewise, the penalty shoot-out failures at the World Cups and European Championships of 1990, 1996, 1998, 2004 and 2006 were disappointing but not decisive.

You would, however, have to add the creation of the Premier League as one of the most important things that has happened to the national game – not least because of the riches England's top clubs have accumulated and the power they now wield.

But, looking at the bigger picture, I would include in the list England's failure to reach the 2008 European Championships – in particular the manner of their defeat to Croatia on 21 November 2007 at the rebuilt Wembley Stadium.

Croatia, a recently war-torn country with a population of just 4 million people, had players with visibly superior skill who nimbly danced their way into a 2-0 lead. England's players recoiled like a wounded boxer smarting from the taste of too many stinging blows. Instinct told them to resort to a time-honoured tactic. Get the ball to David Beckham (so famously ditched by newly appointed national coach Steve McClaren a year earlier) and let old Goldenballs aim wicked crosses at beanpole striker Peter Crouch, in the hope that England's scurrying midfielders could desperately feed off the scraps.

It worked – briefly. Frank Lampard stroked home a penalty and Crouch got his head on to a Beckham cross for the equaliser. But then a long distance skimmer from Mladen Petrić slipped under Scott Carson's outstretched arm and, as Slaven Bilić's team celebrated wildly, English football knew it was time for a rethink. This was a defeat that indicated that all is not well with the national game. The difference between the teams in terms of skill, or 'technical ability' as it is known these days, was palpable and far outweighed the margin of defeat. Should England's campaign have come down to this final group game anyway? Not, you might say, for a major footballing nation.

The media wasted little in delivering a damning verdict on McClaren. Many had not wanted him in the first place – the FA had infamously chased Brazilian coach Luiz Felipe Scolari ahead of the 2006 World Cup, who was deemed a more palatable choice.

'Sorry England Crash Out,' said the *Daily Mail*. 'Outclassed, outfought and out thought,' wrote Henry Winter in the *Daily Telegraph*. Shaun Custis in the *Sun* was even more forthright, 'Useless, pathetic, insipid, spineless, desperate, rubbish and all those other words we are not allowed to print in the nation's favourite newspaper. England are the joke of European football.'

Heinous crimes such as carrying an umbrella and constantly sipping water at the Croatia game didn't help McClaren's cause – he just didn't fit the image of a gaffer who would 'run them' the following morning, chuck tea cups around the dressing room or deliver hair-drying team talks. To many, that was as important as his tactical nous. The FA agreed with the media outcry and McClaren was duly sacked.

Another boot was laid into England's so-called 'Golden Generation' – a phrase unwisely coined by the FA earlier in the decade to include the likes of Beckham, Steven Gerrard, Sol Campbell and Joe Cole who all played in the Croatia match (and to some extent Rio Ferdinand, John Terry and Michael Owen who didn't). They had already received a collective pasting for failing to progress past the quarter-finals of the 2006 World Cup.

But this defeat also revealed a deeper malaise. With the exception of German-raised Owen Hargreaves, who had developed outside the English system, England's younger players like the injured Wayne Rooney for example, or Scott Carson, Micah Richards, Joleon Lescott, Wayne Bridge, Shaun Wright-Phillips, Jermain Defoe and Theo Walcott were players whose skills had been honed within England's elite club academy system which had its ground rules laid out in 1997 in an FA document entitled *A Charter for Quality*. Its architect was the FA's newly appointed technical director, Howard Wilkinson.

The publication of that document – and what it has led to – may yet prove to be one of English football's seismic moments. The charter granted England's top clubs the right to open their own 'academies' and gave them far greater powers than they'd had before. Most importantly the age at which club coaching could start went down from fourteen years old to nine and the number of hours they could be coached was increased from one hour a week to five. The main focus of this book is to examine closely this new set of responsibilities and the wide range of potential welfare concerns that it raises.

The justification for these changes, as always, was said to be the need and desire to produce better players. Though some argued that the real reason was to get the best, most valuable players snapped up as soon as possible and therefore, if you get right down to it, make more money.

By 2008-09, 11 years after the publication of the charter, some 10,000 boys now play in English professional club football academies and centres of excellence each season. But the failure of the national team to reach the European Championships finals in Austria and Switzerland revealed that the charter's expectations – that a blend of the 'golden generation' and this younger breed of academy talent might provide a winning combination for the senior national team – had simply not been met.

This failure to qualify had a bigger impact than the mere wounding of national pride. England's national side had not failed to reach major football finals since the 'do-I-not-like-that' days of Graham Taylor when they missed out on the 1994 World Cup finals. Between 1993 and the Croatia defeat, the prestige of the domestic game had risen inexorably, driven largely by the popularity of the Sky TV-fuelled Premier League, which has attracted a plethora of world-class talent and is now, undisputedly, the world's wealthiest, swankiest league.

English football isn't just sexy and big business – it is now a significant part of the UK economy and had benefited from a seemingly guaranteed biannual summer bonanza between 1996 and 2006, during which time England reached every World Cup and European Championships finals.

The estimated economic impact of failure to reach the 2008 European Championships was £2 billion – a bitter pill to swallow in the teeth of an impending recession. Within days of England's defeat against Croatia share values tumbled and job cuts were announced. Sportswear retailers felt the squeeze instantly. Within a month of the

Croatia defeat Sports Direct International, the company founded by Newcastle United chairman Mike Ashley, which manages the Sports World chain and Lillywhites, announced that profits for the preceding 26 weeks had slumped 35.2% and predicted a grim 2008 following England's elimination from Euro 2008.

A company statement said: "England failing to qualify for the European Championship 2008 will have a material impact on the business ... Umbro has stated that it will now manufacture only 1 million new replica England away shirts rather than 3 million it had originally planned. In addition, we expect sales of other products such as home shirts, shorts, socks, training wear, non-Umbro England products, flags, etc. to be significantly reduced, plus there will be an impact due to the lack of related footfall. Although it is difficult to estimate the impact precisely, our initial assessment is that this will impact ... in the full 2008 calendar year by circa £50m."

In April 2008, rival retailer, JJB, announced the closure of 72 of its 420 UK stores, axing 800 jobs as sales dipped by 28 per cent. Again poor replica kit sales were a key concern. A visit to a local JJB High Street store the week before Euro 2008 began revealed an almost total lack of interest. Instead of being confronted by the usual images of Beckham, Terry, Gerrard and others, the England kits were hidden among the Billy-No-Mates of sportswear at the back of the store.

The British Retail Consortium estimated that the 2006 World Cup generated £1.25 billion with significant chunks spread across several sectors of the economy: £720 million made by the retail industry; £285 million by pubs and £300 million in advertising revenue. Each week the England national team competes in a major international tournament is reckoned to be worth £124 million to the UK licensed trade – with an estimated 815 million pints sold by UK pubs during the 2006 World Cup (an incredible 13 pints for each and every UK citizen), and overall an increase of £60 million on sales during non-football tournament years.

That is a whole lot of responsibility to heap upon England goalkeeper Scott Carson's outstretched hand.

The PFA didn't miss the chance to wade in with its own gloomy audit. Released a few weeks after the Croatia defeat, the dramatically entitled *Meltdown*, a 20-page, 6,000-word report penned for the PFA by journalist Chris Lightbown, focussed largely on the influx of foreign players into English football.

The report made many startling observations about the state of the English game, in particular the Premier League's increasing reliance on foreign players, the decreased opportunities offered to home-grown talent and the knock-on effect for the England national team. Since the inception of the Premier League in 1993 – *Meltdown* revealed – the number of British players in the Premier League had dropped from 462 (90 per cent) to 246 (49 per cent, and only 38 per cent being English) in 2006-07.

The breakdown of home-grown English players in specific positions made even grimmer reading. Just 34 central defenders in 2007 in comparison to 72 in 1993; 16 wingers compared to 36; 93 midfielders reduced to 44; and home-grown goalkeepers, once considered to be England's strongest position, were outnumbered two to one by foreigners in 2006-07.

The report added weight to the concerns raised by respected figures like Sir Trevor Brooking, the FA's head of football development, for years – that English players need not only better opportunities to play but also better coaching. It applauded good practice at clubs so seemingly different as Manchester United and Crewe Alexandra for their stable management and investment in youth development, which, in differing ways, have reaped rewards. 'If two clubs as far apart on the spectrum can make the same formula work, so can those in between,' it reasoned.

The performance of England's national teams at youth and senior level were equally damned. Using a points system from performances at international tournaments, *Meltdown* produced a graph to show just how meagre England's achievements from under-17s to senior level had been, coming 15th among all nations, just behind Turkey and Ukraine and slightly ahead of Nigeria, but well behind the big four – Italy, Brazil, Spain and France – whose scores rocketed far ahead of the rest.

'Hardly the stuff of dreams', the report scoffed, before suggesting that failure to qualify for major tournaments might be something the country will have to grow accustomed to. 'We must act now,' it concluded.

Lack of opportunity is one thing – but the unashamed, overarching concern of this book is the welfare of all the 10,000 boys who play in England's football factories each season – the 99 per cent who don't make it as well as the estimated 1 per cent of boys who do furnish domestic football club first teams and senior international teams, having started their club careers at the age of nine (although boys as young as four and five years old are being recruited to club development centres).

Achieving the dream of playing at the top end of the game is harder than ever – for the reasons *Meltdown* suggested. 'The quality of our graduates hasn't deteriorated,' Mike Foster, general secretary of the Premier League told me. 'It has increased. But the standard they have to reach is higher. The bar has been raised considerably. Genuine home-grown players now have to be world class.'

Overall, professional clubs are to be applauded for the money they invest in youth development – estimated to have been some £66 million a year between the 92 English Premier and Football League clubs in 2005-06. According to Richard Lewis in his 2007 *Review of Young Player Development in Professional Football* (also referred to as the *Lewis Report*), this expenditure – 3.3 per cent of football's turnover – is broadly in line with the sums UK and US companies invest in research and development (which, crudely speaking, is the business equivalent of youth development).

Lewis's report – amazingly the first major review commissioned in the 10 years since the new system allowing professional clubs to coach tens of thousands of children at pre-teen ages for the first time had been devised – came up with 66 recommendations for improvement, from governance through to the quality of coaching.

The sum invested in youth development, however, is dwarfed by the cash slipping into player pockets, rocketing transfer fees and agents' payments as the game has become increasingly reliant on procuring players who can be guaranteed to do a job – indeed often to keep the first-team manager in a job in a profession where the average length of appointment has slid to below 18 months.

While facilities for young players, like those described in this book at Manchester United, Aston Villa and Middlesbrough, were unimaginable 20 years ago, the situation across the 92 league clubs is a mixed bag. According to the *Lewis Report* 75 per cent of Football League clubs claim the grant aid they receive from the FA and the Premier League (worth £180,000 a year) was the most important factor for their youth development programmes. Without it, many would struggle to run academies or centres of excellence.

There is educational funding too, and a number of colleges and universities also run courses to help students derive an income from football, but this is mainly at semi-professional level. The fact is that England's professional clubs have been handed a terrific, almost onerous, responsibility for the development of English football. To do that they are recruiting boys as young as four, who they groom in development centres in preparation for joining the main academies at the age of nine.

Alarmingly, the reason they do so, according to interviewees for this book, is fear – fear of missing out on the next Theo Walcott or Wayne Rooney. But why are they scared? Well, it isn't just about talent – it is about business. It is about getting the best player signed to the club so he will either play for them or they can sell him, or both.

The clubs' aim, spelt out with remarkable clarity by Manchester United's former academy director Les Kershaw in a Radio Five Live programme in 2004, is not to develop players for England's representative teams – they are working exclusively for themselves. 'Ours is a club country,' said Huw Jennings, the Premier League's former head of youth development. The players – the 'raw material' as many football people call them – are seen as little more than commodities. They are made, they are bought and they are sold.

Most boys dream of making it as professional footballers. They see the fame, the wealth, the lifestyle, the fast cars, the glamorous WAGS … and they want a piece of it. Who wouldn't? It is a powerful aphrodisiac when a football club comes knocking at the door and tells you that you are the best thing since sliced bread, and its effect is palpable. For parents, there is no pester power like it. Forget *Doctor Who*, Pokemon cards or fast food – no parent wants to deny his or her son the chance to make it as a footballer because of their own reservations that it might all end in tears. The clubs know it – which is why they get so much acquiescence from parents.

In reality, allowing your son to go down the line of becoming a professional footballer is not an easy decision to take. There are serious doubts that the football industry has truly got to grips with what it can do to the hearts and minds of the young boys it gathers close to its chest, who can sniff the fame and glory but are most likely to be suddenly jettisoned without care and support. And clubs do themselves little credit when dismissing complaints at the way they treat youngsters who fall by the wayside as the gripes of 'pushy parents'.

You have to wonder how fully thought out – and, equally important, how thoroughly implemented – the child protection measures laid out in the *Charter for Quality* have been by some clubs. There are many wonderful people working in youth development – people with a real passion for their work and a real depth of knowledge and understanding, who in some cases are producing fantastic results. It is a pity not enough of them are working together because they share so many similar experiences. This book is not a casual sideswipe at them but it does pause to ask some serious questions.

Sadly, it seems there are coaches and scouts out there who are either misguided or simply so focussed on their task of recruiting and producing players that they fail to view the boys as children (one parent I spoke to felt the boys were seen as 'units'). One development centre coach described a group of six-year-old boys who were no longer required as 'culled'. Another Premier League academy coach recalled the day when a rival coach had volleyed a bucket of water down the touchline because a boy had mis-controlled the ball.

The seemingly endless trading of boys between clubs – described as 'child trafficking' by a representative of the English Schools FA – and the coercion of players and parents by clubs to breech regulations designed for their own welfare must also come into question.

The pressure on youth coaches is exacerbated by a lack of understanding at boardroom level. Off the record (obviously), academy coaches grumble about needing to dig out results in order to keep their jobs – largely because of the chairman's ego when scanning the weekend's academy results and a failure to appreciate the embracing priority of youth development. Developing players for the future, seemingly, comes second to getting good results now.

The parents and children interviewed for this book are a mere smattering of the 10,000 or more players swilling through England's elite football system each season. They are quoted in order to relay their experiences as a whole, not just the disappointment of being released. Their voices deserve to be heard. The same goes for teachers, academics and grass roots coaches. Few of the interviewees wanted to name specific clubs and it would be unfair to do so for many reasons. There are also no comments in this book about the playing ability of boys. Football is, above all, a game of opinions. Coaches have to make tough decisions. It is, without any shadow of a doubt, the hardest job in youth football.

Despite the time, effort and huge investment that has gone into England's newfound youth development schemes, one thing the clubs, their leagues and the FA haven't been very good at is finding out what the people who have been through the system felt about it. 'We hold our hands up. We haven't done enough,' Mike Foster, general secretary of the Premier League, admitted.

That is quite some revelation. The Secretary of State for Culture, Media and Sport, Andy Burnham, who, like so many other parents, puts the nets up for his son's team in Warrington on Saturday mornings believes, 'Football needs to have a long, hard look at itself and ask if it is doing right by those young people because the pound signs are there when they are a potential asset and they should accept the responsibility that goes with it.' He added, 'Youth development is what supporters expect. They want to see young talent coming through. It is a good thing.'

At its best youth development is magnificent. It forms a unique bond between clubs, their supporters and their local communities. But children are not the chattels of football clubs. As Tony Whelan, the thoughtful and erudite architect of Manchester United's pioneering junior coaching programme said, 'You only get one chance at being a boy. The time they spend with us should be the happiest days of their lives.'

Similarly, Howard Wilkinson, architect of the document which revamped youth development in England, said in his 1997 charter, 'The central figure ... is the player and his (or her) best interests.

Attempting to provide quality experiences for all young players at all levels is the overriding principle.'

It would be marvellous to be able to tell the story of England's unmitigated success in transforming the rags of a once dilapidated youth policy into the finest production line of sublime, silky skilled talent world football has ever seen, whose players flow like a steady stream of cream into club first teams at all levels – and that England's national teams were winning trophies with repeated monotony. But you can't because that is not the case.

Although it's undoubtedly true that English football clubs are producing technically better players than they were, so they should be. The boys train in better facilities, for longer and have far more knowledge of diet, nutrition, physiology and psychology than their predecessors and are monitored constantly (indeed part of their education is now to actively participate in monitoring their own progress), not to mention access to computer-aided post-match performance analysis.

But part of the overall picture is that actually we all need to back off – to let kids play, not necessarily play football, just play – in order to let them develop the building blocks of sport, obtain physical literacy – the abilities to run, jump and catch – and the physical and mental flexibility just to have fun and enjoy playing sport rather than it being a means to an end. These issues are dealt with in more detail in Chapter 11. This book is intended to serve as a guide to parents who won't necessarily understand what taking their son to an academy really means, and uses real experiences to explain what will really take place, unlike the glossy pamphlets, prospectuses and brochures produced by the clubs themselves.

Furthermore, there are serious questions to be asked of the game's main stakeholders in elite youth development, who are at loggerheads over the control and direction of this system. It is arguably a power struggle between the traditional governors of the national game (the FA) and, in monetary terms, the new guv'nors (the Premier League), with the cap-in-hand body representing the other 72 professional clubs, the Football League, sandwiched somewhere in between – all three fighting a turf war. How about fighting for the well-being of kids first and foremost?

Some of the new ideas are supposedly based on youth development systems at top European clubs. However, are England's private football clubs (increasingly owned outright by global businessmen) really comparable with continental models of club ownership and their direct links to the regional and national sports infrastructures and grass roots communities? Probably not.

England is a unique footballing country and few can argue against the amount of excitement engendered in stadiums up and down the country every week. Even arch critics of youth development in England, like Bert-Jan Heijmans, a Dutch football coach doing some remarkable grass roots work in the north-east of England, is enthralled by the passion and the pace of English football. For all the technical mastery of players in his homeland, actually, when push comes to shove, 'BJ' prefers to watch a full-blooded English encounter.

But why does the 'Pitch to Podium' Sport England model – calculated to be 10,000 hours of quality time an elite athlete needs to spend preparing for success – have to be taught solely by professional football clubs from as early an age as possible?

Why is the trawl for talent so widespread in English football? By definition, elite youth development is designed to weed out the ones who won't be good enough. It is a selection process. Do we really have 10,000 elite young footballers in with a shout of becoming professionals? Only a relative handful will make it each year. What happens to the rest of them?

What are the consequences of taking a boy aged six, telling him he is going to become a professional footballer, then crushing those dreams and telling him he's not wanted when he fails to make the grade? Such a disappointment will have an inevitable effect on his social and educational development, and not just for schoolboys, but for full-time apprentices between the ages of 16 and 18. This is a serious business. Boys will always be boys. They will slip behind with their education – they will underachieve and won't make the best of themselves. (At this point, it is important to stress that this book does not undermine or dismiss women's or girls' football, it is just that the primary focus is on professional football and at present that means the men's game in England.)

The problems were foreseeable – and there have been too many stories of failure, since the publication of Howard Wilkinson's *Charter for Quality*. This book is partly the result of research and reports carried out over many years, in particular the years since the charter. The key issue that has arisen as a result of all this research is the lack of connection between those instigating changes and the people affected by the policies put in place. It is here that we find the roots of why we are getting things so badly wrong in football and other sports in the UK.

One area football's authorities have prevaricated over for too long is the inspection and monitoring of academies and centres of excellence – and the publication of this information. There is talk of an independent standards unit being introduced. This is overdue and much needed, so that parents can make informed choices on whether to send their children to a football academy, and if so, which one may suit them best. With respect to the clubs, the experience of a six-week trial is not the same as the assessment of an Ofsted-style report.

Although they often don't know it, parents have more power than they think. Clubs sometimes say that parents must sign up on behalf of their sons at the age of nine or they will otherwise be rejected forever. But the fact is that if a youngster is seen as good enough, he will be signed up at whatever age he is spottted.

Though they have no right, some clubs push their luck by trying to prevent boys from participating in school sport. They cite the risk of overplay. But why do they assume their right of priority? Is the sacrifice of not playing for a school or local community club team worth spending up to eight hours or more on the road driving to an away academy game only to play 30 minutes of football?

A report called *The Good Childhood Inquiry*, commissioned by the Children's Society and released in January 2009, found that British children were the unhappiest in Europe. The report concluded that children's lives in Britain have become 'more difficult than in the past', adding that 'more young people are anxious and troubled'. Is football heaping its own undue pressure on to the shoulders of boys who should be learning to love sport and not focussing on strutting their stuff to the satisfaction of a football club?

The FA is only now preparing age-appropriate coaching courses for academies and centres of excellence. Why wasn't this done ages ago? As a country we have fewer qualified coaches than most other leading European nations. Many of our top managers avoid obtaining the required qualifications, viewing them only as mandatory requirements and not something they should willingly want. However, they would actually help to make managers better coaches and, more importantly, would help the players they are coaching.

Perhaps the hardest thing to accept is that research suggests that some boys are so put off by the experience of being pursued by football clubs at such a young age, of being intensely coached and ultimately disappointed at having tried their guts out and failed to make the grade, that they lose their appetite to play the game at all – maybe even falling out of love with sport altogether.

Let's get down to brass tacks. In a country where teenage obesity is rocketing off the index scale (a 2007 British Medical Council report found that more than 1 million under-16 year olds in the UK were classified as obese), boys who have been identified as talented footballers are giving up on sport as a result of their experiences in elite football developments centres. This is truly worrying.

There is nothing wrong in chasing dreams – except that too often in football for many boys it is like chasing a bubble. The closer they get to it, the further it floats away from their grasp and when they reach out ... it just bursts in their hands and vanishes.

This book examines where English football is going wrong and asks what can be done to ensure that the boys chasing those tantalising dreams can do so in a healthy, beneficial way rather than one that appears to have little regard for their well-being when their dreams don't become a reality.

CHAPTER 2

GOLDEN DAYS AND GOLDEN GENERATIONS

If there was a golden age when England's national team
dominated the world, can you tell me when it was because
I think I missed it?

Huw Jennings, ex-head of youth development at the FA Premier League

The trouble with nostalgia is that it isn't what it used to be. There is a mistaken view that there was once a golden age of English football – a time when England produced loads of world-class players and all was well with the beautiful game. England's golden period is reckoned to be the 1950s – an era when a plethora of home-grown talent cheered the hearts of record post-war crowds, most notably the Busby Babes, Stan Cullis's Wolves and local folklore heroes like Jackie Milburn, Tommy Lawton, Tom Finney and Stanley Matthews.

But the sad fact is that, internationally, no matter how conversely depressed or buoyant people feel about the international team now – the England senior team has bounced along pretty much where it always has for most of the time it has been involved in international competition. Apart from a few appearances in quarter-finals and semi-finals, all we have to show for over 130 years of international competition is one World Cup, a tournament won in formulaic fashion in 1966 by Alf Ramsey's wingless wonders.

In truth there has never really been a merry time when England knocked out a Terracotta Army of perfectly formed footballers capable of taking on the world. There was never a comprehensive, fully funded national programme supported by the clubs designed to do this. Stretching way back to the game's professional origins, there has never been a big idea on how to develop home-grown talent.

Yet the myth of youth weighs heavily in football. Developing players from the local areas to feed into clubs and becoming a representation of them – pushing them forward, straining every sinew; 'wanting it more' because they were local lads and understood what the club means to fans – is part of the game's mythology. It conjures up images of the local football club as some kind of organic institution with players who are home-grown, locally produced, 'sourced' even from local leagues, as one interviewee suggested.

Locality is a key aspect of a football club, something that makes it special. The character of a club, except for a handful in the top flight, still comes from its local support base. The owners might put the money in, but they are only symbolically in charge – football clubs are community institutions. They belong, spiritually, to the fans – however much this idea has been tested in recent years by Premier League clubs with owners, managerial staff and playing squads assembled from many countries and continents.

Of course, this is nothing new. From the very start of professional football the game has shipped in players from afar. Initially it was Scottish migrant footballers heading south for jobs in the factories of the industrial north and the Midlands who would turn out at weekends for their adopted home-town clubs. They were paid for their services, pushing local lads out of the picture as teams went in pursuit of results, trophies and league titles. In essence, how different were they from today's top earners who fly in from all points of the globe?

Traditionally, youth development, as with many other aspects of English football, tended to stagger forward in its own merry old way. Development programmes weren't on most club radars. Proverbially, they whistled down mines, recruiting players from local leagues and fellow clubs. They didn't develop schoolboy talent and wouldn't – indeed couldn't – sign boys until they had left school, so what would have been the point? They simply watched what went on in local school football and signed the best players when they left. Oh, and you didn't have to pay transfer fees for them. Simple.

They were often more than happy to pay their dues with a donation to the local district schools association for 'goodwill' when they signed a youth player. Let's face it, they needed future player's names and contact details – so it made good sense to keep them sweet. But at least the money was ploughed back into the game.

The idea of nurturing talent only gradually dawned on the game. The history of youth development is often linked to hard times and desperation. When all is said and done, when the money has dried up to pay professional players, you can always field 'the kids'. It still happens today.

The club credited with developing the first real nationwide youth development policy is Manchester United, and you can trace its presence right through the club's illustrious history. Back in the 1930s, United weren't the biggest club in the world. They weren't even the biggest team in Manchester. At best they were a yo-yo club between Divisions One and Two and they skated perilously close to going out of business altogether. In 1938, under pressure from supporters to select more local players, they started a scheme devised by club secretary Walter Crickmer and chairman James Gibson called the Manchester United Junior Athletic Club (the MUJACs as they became known), to talent spot the best young players in Lancashire.

'It was revolutionary,' says Tony Whelan, United's Assistant Academy Director and author of *Birth of the Babes: Manchester United Youth Policy, 1950-57*. 'The idea for the MUJACs came up at a board meeting in 1937 and it was formed in 1938. It was a youth set-up – junior teams playing in local leagues. Most teams at the time were full of seasoned professionals. The idea of having young boys playing in your first team or having a youth policy just wasn't something that was considered. Clubs didn't have coherent youth policies – to get kids in at a young age from school, develop them and get them into the first team – it was completely new.'

United's major rivals in youth development terms were Wolverhampton Wanderers. Manager Frank Buckley, had already put a scheme in place at his previous club Blackpool before doing the same at Molineux following his appointment in 1927. Both United and Wolves gathered together the threads of those fledgling pre-war policies and, along with Vic Buckingham, visionary coach at West Bromwich Albion who later managed Ajax and developed the Dutch concept of 'total football', became the main drivers of youth development in the 1950s, Busby, with his 'Babes', Cullis' with his 'Cubs'.

Again the clubs' motivation was desperation – there wasn't any money around and they needed new players to replace those who'd lost their lives or their best years to the war. 'Matt Busby had the wisdom and foresight to take the basic foundation of the MUJAC and drive it on in a remarkable way,' said Whelan. 'They got some scouts – not a lot, just eight or nine – but they were the best and they scoured the country looking for talent.'

The boys came directly into the club at 15 years old. You couldn't sign until you left school. It was actually illegal to sign any earlier. 'They brought them up and nurtured them. A lot of the impetus for that was Matt Busby's own upbringing. He lost his father in the First World War and Matt became the breadwinner. He helped his mother out so, in many ways, he saw the Busby Babes as his surrogate family. His own experiences as a player for Manchester City and Liverpool hadn't been great so I think he wanted better for the boys who came through the club – to ensure they would be treated properly. He had a deep sense of family and caring for players.'

Other clubs continued to recruit players in time-honoured fashion. 'The schools football system was much more dynamic and strong than it is now,' said Whelan. 'Players came through the schools. They were the academies of those days. Clubs picked up the best boys from schools football.'

Other clubs developed their own players so that they could use them as cheap ground staff, doing menial low paid jobs around the ground. Recruitment wasn't a particularly noble business. Charming your way in through the front door was a key skill. Competition was fierce. Signing the best players was a cut-throat business – it wasn't uncommon for prospective players' parents to receive an unexpected visit from a man in a brown coat delivering white goods for the kitchen.

But by setting up their youth development programme Manchester United stole a march on their rivals. Their chief scout was Joe Armstrong. His son, also called Joe Armstrong, also a United scout, still uses advice passed down to him by his father. 'He'd say, "Do what you think, and tell them after," said Joe junior. 'Being tactful and pleasant helped. There was a lot of visiting done in those days.' Armstrong senior was known as Uncle Joe to Bobby Charlton's family and other players he brought to United. His was a key role – and he did better than the rest. Where did he look for players? 'Local district and county schools football.'

Schools football was relatively free of intervention from the professional game back then and was well funded, particularly in the postwar era when consensus politics was about developing a future. The public funding of school sport has a long tradition dating back to Victorian Britain and the concerns of doctors and benefactors to politicians for the health of Britain's working class industrial poor ensured that Physical Education (PE) became part of the school curriculum. Football was to play a key role.

At his soccer centres Bobby Charlton used to hold a ball aloft and declare it as the 'greatest toy ever invented'. Football – the game of the masses – played a key part in PE. Few kids needed motivation to play football and engage in the essentials of sport. They'd eagerly chase the ball, run, dribble, tackle, apply quick-thinking nous to manoeuvre their way out of tight situations, use balance and co-ordination or simply run off steam.

The English Schools Football Association (ESFA) was formed in 1904 to oversee inter-schools, district, county, national and international regulation and competition. It developed into a reasonably prosperous business, with its crown jewels being the annual Under-15 Schoolboys international between England and Scotland, which often attracted full houses of 100,000 at Wembley in the post-war era (plenty enough to swell the ESFA's coffers). The crowd comprised mainly boisterous kids bussed in from all corners of the country – coach trips organised as a thank you by schools and county associations – on what would now be known as a bonding or team-building exercise. The matches were screened on ITV's *World of Sport*.

Those halcyon days raised revenue that was wholesomely ploughed back into schools football.

Little by little, professional clubs began to sign and train school-boys – until they were headed off by the Football Association, alarmed at the development of something outside of its control. Indeed it could be argued that this threat dragged the game's much maligned govern-ing body into the modern era after the Second World War. The FA had only produced its first coaching manual in 1936 – a document penned by committee with virtually no representation from anyone coaching in the professional game, although future England manager Walter Winterbottom was one of the authors.

While the likes of Busby, Cullis and Buckingham were forging ahead with youth development and devising tactics to take on the best clubs in Europe, the FA would only employ Winterbottom as England senior team manager as long as he agreed to bundle the role in with heading the FA coaching department.

Remarkably, coaching in principle, let alone as a means to an end (i.e. to produce better players), had been opposed by some at the FA. Administrators who governed the game, many of whom had barely soiled their shoes by stepping foot on a training ground, preferred to purport their own rule of thumb and homespun theory that players needed to bulk up on bully beef and chips prior to kick off and that starving players of time with the ball would make them 'want it' more on matchdays.

Even though the FA is a vastly modernised sports governing body, it is only now just getting round to recognising the need to design elite, age-specific coach education courses. Fellow football-mad countries had forged ahead with this in the 1960s – stirred on by clubs who embedded themselves deeply into the local community sport – by creating sophisticated coaching structures and putting thousands upon thousands of coaches through courses of all kinds so that they could develop and nurture young talent.

For the most part, English clubs have always acted as 'nickers and pinchers' of the best talent, which is all these privately owned enter-prises have ever aspired to do – creaming off the best players for their own private gain.

Whereas the British game fed off an immense appetite and enthusiasm among its spectators, in countries such as Holland football was taught at community clubs and built around active participation in clubs with grass roots structures. Many continental clubs have hundreds of players in dozens of teams organised by tens of coaches and support staff. They learn how to do their job properly. Players get time on the ball, coaches know how to coach, support staff know how to do their jobs. They are all part of the club – they have clubhouses – places to meet and discuss tactics and issues and build a club ethos. They also have formal and direct links with elite clubs – with paths for the progression of talented players. The cream floats to the top.

How many grass roots football clubs like this exist in England, let alone those professional players? Other than the odd ad hoc arrangement, Britain's private elite clubs have rarely bothered to forge such formal structures. They have rarely looked at working together with the organisers of schools, district, regional and national schools football and, for that matter, company sport, which was also once a rich source of talent – for not all players shone in schools football.

Up until the mid-1960s boys left school at 15 and went out to work. A familiar hunting ground for clubs, therefore, was company sport. Once the bedrock of British sport, it has withered away to the point of virtual non-existence today with some of the strongest leagues, in West London, Birmingham, Manchester and Newcastle, folding in the 2000s.

So how do you get to join your local team? Let's take an average footballer from the 1960s and 1970s. Mick Evans enjoyed a long spell in the game with Oxford United, Walsall, Swansea and Crewe before injury ended his professional career – although he carried on for a few more seasons with Worcester City, Redditch United and Malvern Town.

Born in 1946, Evans grew up in 1950s West Bromwich. 'I always played for my school team, Christchurch Primary School,' he recalled. He remembers his home-town club Albion reaching the 1954 FA Cup final – deep-lying centre forward Ronnie Allen was his childhood hero – but playing rather than watching took over. He played 11-a-side junior school football, frowned upon and rightly so today, from the age of nine, and was a regular in his secondary school at the Technical High School.

Recreational teams did not exist and scouts limited their interest to district schools matches. Although Evans played a handful of games for West Bromwich boys, regulars like Clive Ford (Wolves) and Selwyn Vale (West Bromwich Albion) were snared by local club talent spotters and, at 15, were whisked off to join their respective club's ground staff. 'They would train in the morning and then spend the rest of the day doing chores like sweeping stands and dressing rooms, cleaning boots and helping the groundsman,' remembers Evans.

An engineering apprenticeship awaited Mick Evans – and he got the job through playing football for the works team while still at school. 'Back then all the big works had their own sports facilities – it was a big thing,' recalls Evans. 'They wanted to promote themselves, which worked if the team was near the top of the table.'

Evans then spent two years at a factory in Tipton called Vono – catching the bus from West Bromwich to make a 7.30 a.m. start. At weekends, he played for the factory in the Welfare League, a youth division of the Birmingham Works and District League – the largest works league in England. At its peak the league boasted 280 teams playing in 20 divisions in a region once known as the 'workshop of the world'. Founded by the instigator of the Football League, Aston Villa chairman William McGregor, it folded in 2000 with just seven teams left.

At the factory, Evans remembers, it was hard work, 'I was doing a bit of graft and bending pipes – you had to be strong'. At weekends the by-now 5 foot 11 inches tall and 11½ stone striker had a punishing schedule of matches on Saturday mornings, Saturday afternoons and Sunday mornings. But it worked out and he was selected to play for the Welfare League representative team.

The Welfare League, like similar local leagues, was heavily scouted (roughly 20 per cent of players were recruited in this way by professional clubs during the era) and Evans was spotted by Oxford United and went on trial. 'I scored,' he recalls with a smile, and he made journeys back and forth for midweek training, returning on the milk train between Oxford and Birmingham in the early hours.

'Vono weren't best pleased', he recalls. They didn't want to lose a prized player. But Oxford decided not to sign him so Evans carried on learning the fineries of pipe bending. At the start of the following season, a colleague at the factory got Evans a trial with Walsall FC. Again he scored and this time he signed amateur terms and was selected to play for the Birmingham County youth team. This included a host of players already signed to Football League clubs, including Wolves goalkeeper Phil Parkes, David Rudge of Aston Villa and Cardiff winger Gary Bell, all of whom would go on to have distinguished careers.

For six months he carried on with his apprenticeship, trained with Walsall on Tuesday and Thursday evenings and played weekend matches for their youth side, the A team (the club's third team) and the reserves. The youth team was made up of amateurs like Evans, and ground staff players (including later Leeds United and England striker Allan Clarke). At the end of the season he received a letter from the club – with a footnote casually asking him to drop by to discuss professional terms. 'There wasn't much discussion, I was told I'd get £14 a week and a £20 signing on fee.'

As a pro, he played alongside older players in the reserve team. 'I learned a lot from them – they showed you what to do,' said Evans. 'Modern players miss that. You learned from playing with better play-ers. It was a bit like work really – you learned from guys who can do it – and that was my youth development.'

Evans made his league debut at the age of 19, and became a virtual ever-present for the following seven seasons. Walsall then sold him to Swansea City, managed by former 'Busby Babe' Harry Gregg, for £6,000. After three seasons at Vetch Field, Gregg moved on to Crewe and Evans followed. But a year later, at 31, he picked up a back injury that ended his Football League career. After a season at non-League Worcester City his career wound down at Redditch and Malvern. Afterwards Evans went back into engineering to make the most of what he had learned before starting his football career.

Although it was not a glorious career in terms of cups and trophies, Evans's story is a good one and typical of his era. He was able to enjoy a long career in football without being spotted at school and was picked up early by a professional club. He played football in his teens for fun with his mates and more seriously for his school, company, district and county and was free to go on trial at successive professional clubs without having to sign on the dotted line as soon as he crossed the threshold of the first club he visited. Most importantly he learned a trade he could return to if his football career failed.

Not everyone had such a happy experience. Many youth players were treated appallingly by their clubs and were used as little more than skivvies, and inevitably were hopelessly overplayed.

As the post-war consensus faded in the late 1970s, traditional apprenticeships bit the dust along with much of the nation's established industry. With it came the decline of company sport and the thrust of Thatcherism ('there's no such thing as society'), which heralded a massive decline in council-run sports facilities – rate-capped into submission and forced to tender pitch maintenance to the lowest bidder (usually a firm who would cut the grass and mark the line rather than actually attend to the pitch).

School sport, like much of the rest of society in the shared cross-party social and political values in the post-war era, was reasonably well funded and enthusiastically overseen by PE teachers who were so sufficiently motivated and proud of their boys that they willingly gave over their free time to after-school coaching and Saturday morning matches. The clubs dipped into schoolboy coaching and the FA ran regional centres of excellence – but in 1984 English football's governing body decided to proceed with a big and bold adventure.

The National Sports Centre at Lilleshall Hall in Shropshire cuts an imposing image for the first-time visitor. The tree-lined driveway alone is roughly a mile long. Originally built in 1831 as the hunting lodge and family retreat of the Duke of Sutherland, today Lilleshall is a flagship residential training centre and an award-winning National Centre of Excellence for many of the UK's top sportsmen and women. It is secluded – the nearest town is about five miles away.

It was within these leafy confines that the Football Association National School ran from 1984 to 1999. Some 220 boys aged between 14 and 16 attended the school in that time, combining the final two years of their secondary school education with intense football coaching.

Often living within a media bubble (the press were naturally fascinated by this newfound football finishing school), it wasn't designed to replicate their home environment. It was a football academy with the boys living in. 'They were selected for their ability to cope with the surroundings and to benefit from the education on offer', said Tony Pickerin, who was principal at the school for nine years, in an interview in 2004.

Even among this handpicked group of players only 25 per cent went on to sign professional contracts at 18. Pickerin, who became head of the FA's Education and Child Protection department and, later, the governing body's Ethics and Sports Equity unit before retiring in 2005, said there can be many reasons why boys at that age don't go on to make it as professional footballers. 'For some it is physical growth or injuries. Others just don't develop as footballers or aren't deemed skilful enough or have the characteristics their club coaches are seeking. Some just lose heart and decide it just isn't for them.'

The FA National School provided the players with the best available sports science back-up at the time – they built an elite programme of football development around school life. It set modest aims – hoping to develop just one player per year through to international level from an average intake of 16 boys. Broadly speaking it achieved its target. But it was an expensive project with the FA investing more than £500,000 a year – funds, argued the ESFA and others, that could have been better spent supporting a wider base of players at regional centres.

A glance through the commemorative brochure produced to mark the closing of the centre shows how few of these handpicked boys made it in professional football. The likes of Michael Owen, Joe Cole, Sol Campbell, Jermain Defoe, Jamie Carragher, Scott Parker, Wes Brown, Trevor Sinclair, Andy Cole, Nick Barmby, Francis Jeffers, Michael Ball and Ben Thatcher have all played senior international football, but these players were the exception, not the rule.

Lilleshall's opulent surroundings provide some illustrative lessons. Even when selecting the pick of the country's 14-year-old players the football world wasn't necessarily at their feet. While another 20 or so played regular Premier League football, including Stuart Taylor, Stuart Parnaby, Neil Clement, Gavin McCann, Ronnie Wallwork, Dean Kiely, Garry Flitcroft, John Ebbrell, Graham Stuart, Mark Robins, Andy Myers, Jon Harley, Jody Morris and Simon Charlton, these players only represent, roughly, a quarter of the lads who went to Lilleshall. Most simply drifted out of the game. Others, like Newcastle United and England's Alan Smith, quit the school to return to his home-town of Leeds (where he joined his local club, Leeds United) because they found living away from home in goldfish-bowl intensity too tough.

On the other hand, West Bromwich Albion defender Neil Clement, who attended the school between 1993 and 1995, loved it. 'I can't speak highly enough of the National School,' Clement said in an interview in 2006. 'It was a strict regime but it was what I needed. It toughened me up and made me a confident person'. Clement's contemporaries included Jody Morris, who joined him on the Youth Training Scheme (YTS) at Chelsea, while his former Baggies' team-mate, Ronnie Wallwork, was in the year above, with Michael Owen in the year below. 'Everyone knew he was going to be special,' said Clement.

Although Clement didn't make it at Chelsea, he moved to West Brom in 2000 where he has achieved his ambition of playing Premier League football. 'The National School gave me an edge. We'd grown up faster than other footballers.'

One of those who fell by the wayside was Craig Gaunt, who attended the school between 1987 and 1989. Born in the Nottinghamshire town of Sutton-in-Ashfield, he went though district, regional then national trials alongside goalkeeper Jonathan Stranger, also from Sutton. 'It was difficult at first. I'd never been away from home before,' recalled Gaunt. The boys were educated at a local secondary school in nearby Shifnal. 'We were loved by the girls and hated by some of the jealous boys,' he recalls. Star players in Gaunt's intake were Trevor Sinclair and Garry Flitcroft, who remain friends. No one else in their cohort made it as players. Stranger eventually became a players' agent and has now left the game completely.

On leaving Lilleshall, the future looked bright for Craig. He joined Arsenal, initially as a trainee then as a professional for three years. He played 90 reserve games but never made the step-up to the first team and drifted back to the Midlands where he has played for several non-league clubs. He isn't bitter. 'The National School was a great grounding. It enabled me to play football in countries like Singapore and the USA which probably wouldn't have happened if I hadn't gone to Lilleshall.'

Initially the school turned out players who became solid professionals, like Mark Robins and Graham Stuart. But as the scheme developed with experience things got better and a number of top performers, like Michael Owen, Joe Cole and Jermain Defoe, emerged.

Some clubs prevented boys who were signed to them from attending the National School, scared that they would meet players from rival clubs and want to leave. But others had monitored its success and wanted a piece of the action. They felt the existing club centre of excellence rules were too restrictive in terms of the time they had to work with school-age players.

English football altered dramatically at the top level of the game with the formation of the Premier League in 1993. The top clubs had broken away from the FA and were filling their pockets with the proceeds (the first BSkyB TV deal was worth £300 million to Premier League clubs). They were also gaining a substantial say in the running of the game, taking seats on the FA's notorious array of influential committees and subcommittees, which meant that they could shape policy. One suggestion was that the National School be rolled out club-by-club.

The situation was resolved in 1997 when Howard Wilkinson joined the FA as its technical director. After a few months in office he announced that the residential FA National School was to close in favour of club academies where boys of primary school age upwards could train part time. Wilkinson wanted to make English players as 'technically proficient' as their continental counterparts, who, he argued, spent more time with their clubs, so became better players. His top-line target was to provide high quality players for the England senior team. 'Some boys were playing more than 100 games a season,' said Wilkinson. 'They had no time to train.' At fault, he thought, were the multiple-level demands on them at school, town, county, club and international level.

One way to reduce the number of games they were expected to play was to limit games played for school, district or with county representative teams. Those elite schoolboy footballers who play in club academies by and large no longer compete in schools football. As a consequence the prominence of schools football has declined and the role of the ESFA has diminished. The FA offered them £1.5 million for its prize asset – the England Schoolboys Under-15s team and consequently took it under their wing. Today, their games, comprising of players from club academy teams who are usually prevented from playing for their schools and for district representative teams, are screened on subscription TV – a filler in the expanded football schedule, and watched by far fewer people with embarrassing gratuitous name-drops by commentators for the clubs the boys are contracted to. Large corporations who have scooped the talent and loaned it back as they see fit.

Today the ESFA is a marginalised, slimmed-down structure – still running inter-schools football with district and county associations, administering a massive network of volunteers who work with 20,000 schools, and delivering a school football programme for boys and girls from under-11 through to under-19. Sometimes it dips into its England schoolboys cash, but generally the ESFA has to find funds from commercial partners. The Premier League writes an annual cheque, as does the FA. Coca Cola, via its fruit juice drink, Minute Maid, sponsors the national boys and girls Under-13s Cup – the largest competition of its kind in Europe with 40,000 children taking part in the 2008-09 season for instance – but it is not what it was. The elite players are signed to the clubs.

The split caused mixed feelings and the wrestling of consciences among school sport coaches. When the club academies opened many, albeit with heavy hearts, opted, understandably, for the golden horizon and kissed goodbye to the hassle of school teaching – the diminishing facilities, poor maintenance of pitches and reduced budgets. They accepted the king's shilling.

Those who left the ESFA included the last England Schoolboys Under-15s manager before the split, Dave Parnaby, who became Middlesbrough's academy director; Dave Bushell, who became head of education and welfare at Manchester United and Paul Brackwell who had a similar role at Aston Villa. Huw Jennings, an Oxfordshire schoolteacher who taught drama and English and was a part-time youth coach with Oxford United, accepted the academy director's job at Southampton FC.

Others stayed to keep the ESFA afloat – but were under no illusions. The clubs have circumvented what was once the main provider of football talent in the country. Today, by the time boys reach secondary school, the best footballers have already been snapped up by the clubs.

Dave Woollaston, an ESFA council member for East Anglia since 1991, has taught at Icknield High School in Luton since completing his teacher training in 1973. He remains dedicated to teaching. 'It is that little bit of flair in a child's eyes. It could be on a football field, it could be in a gymnasium, it could be the kid that can't do a particular maths problem. It is a smile, it's the thought that every child can do something that is important ... I love my job'.

Woollaston devotes some weekends and holiday time to working as an ESFA coach with the England Schools Under-18 squad. Sometimes he coaches at Lilleshall, far away from the action at professional club matches and the hubbub of Icknield High. These boys, though, are not the ones the Sky Sports commentators are bubbling over. They are, as Woollaston notes with due respect, 'the best of the rest,' the pick of the players the professional clubs don't want. 'Most have been with professional clubs but have been released,' he explains.

They are not the 'golden generation' of Beckham, Gerrard, Lampard and co. who belonged to the school sport era – as did all the previous great names of English football. Today's club academy players rarely go near the England Schools set-up, although Theo Walcott, surprisingly, slipped under the radar of academy scouts and played for his school. 'They were on Associated Schoolboy forms and attended FA regional centres,' explains Woollaston. 'But not anymore.'

As far as the Premier League clubs are concerned, the split was necessary. 'What needs to be remembered is where we were 10 years ago,' said Mike Foster, general secretary of the Premier League, 'Professional clubs could only get involved with elite players at the age of 14 and then only for a limited amount of time each week.

'There were complaints about overplay and the impact that was having on young players. We also felt there was also a need for the best players to be put in touch with the best coaches.'

Put simply, the clubs believed they could do it better and wanted more time with the players. 'We were insistent that we must live up to our responsibility to make sure the players were being developed and coached in a suitable environment,' says Foster. 'And we think clubs have lived up to those standards.'

Some people in the professional game wonder whether the bridges need to be rebuilt between the clubs and the ESFA. 'We have been having meetings with the ESFA because when the *Charter for Quality* was brought in it did leave a vacuum in terms of schools football because players were migrating to clubs and obviously the ESFA are concerned about that,' said Jim Briden, youth development business manager for the Football League. 'It is moving slowly,' he added. 'But it needs to happen because, on the outside looking in, if the boys are not given the opportunity to play in that domain then the standard of football is going to suffer and that cannot be good for the game's development long term.'

In truth, the move towards club academies in place of the FA National School and the dramatically reduced role of the English Schools FA was not a replacement measure. It was a new concept in English football. Clubs were granted far greater powers than before. They could recruit boys between nine and 19 years of age and run their academies primarily in the best interests of the clubs. This has not necessarily been in the best interests of the national game nor, say some, at all in the best interests of children. It has bred ferocious competition among clubs to sign up the best boys as young as possible and has had a profound impact on the way English football develops its talent.

CHAPTER 3

HOWARD'S WAY:
THE CHARTER FOR QUALITY

Academy 1 a place of study or training in a special field.
2 a society or institution of distinguished scholars, artists or scientists that aims to promote and maintain standards in its field.
3 a US and Scottish secondary school.

The small Gloucestershire town of Cirencester seems like the last place in Britain to start a revolution – let alone one linked to an activity like football, which is usually associated with urban pride and passion. Although it was the second largest town in Roman Britannia, peering through the town centre's estate agent windows, today it seems that property prices indicate this much sought-after quarter of the Cotswolds, sitting just north of the M4 corridor, is more a favoured haunt of middle-class, metropolitan second-homers escaping to the country. There are plenty of working-class poor around here – they just don't populate the cover of *Cotswold Life*. Yet it is in this unlikely setting that England's first football academy was devised. Not that the FA or England's elite professional clubs would care to admit it, but what happened here was a simple solution to a local problem.

Back in the mid-1990s Cirencester Town FC were non-League small fry – they still are. Even after building a new 4,500 capacity stadium in 2002 with fantastic corporate and community sport facilities, including three full-size and four junior pitches, their first team is lucky to attract 200 spectators to home matches.

Built with a huge slice of cash from the Football Foundation, football's grant-giving charity arm, and the proceeds of the sale of their old ground, Cirencester's Corinium Stadium resembles a continental community club. It is much more about playing and participating than watching – it is an active part of the local community – something the club has carefully nurtured since charting a new course.

Back in 1996 Cirencester's former and far less salubrious home on Tetbury Road was little more than a muddy bog with changing rooms, a bar and basic facilities. Like most clubs at their level, they couldn't afford to splash out on players who, at best, could only take them a temporary step forward.

Instead they embarked on a more visionary mission, shaped by the club's committee, which included England national team masseur Steve Slattery, and current Cirencester Town chairman, Steve Abbley. One part of the mission was to stimulate interest in the development of youth football via a new venture being promoted by the FA called Mini Soccer, a small-sided game for children initially devised as a fun introduction to football (today it is anything but – with teams in leagues and adults urging kids to hunt down trophies, largely, it must be said, to satisfy their own egos.) However, Cirencester's other idea, simple in theory, was to develop their own programme for 16- to 18-year-old players.

By funding a full-time coach to train the players each day, their soccer education could be balanced with academic studies, provided just across the road at Cirencester College, a recently formed tertiary college which, in 1991, had taken over the sixth form at the adjacent Deer Park School.

Ambitions were high that the novelty of the scheme could attract better players from a 60-mile radius. Being coached at Cirencester Town rather than, say, a Premier League club, meant that no one was likely to be confused by what was on offer or the likely outcome of their football education.

Most of the recruits to the scheme had been rejected by professional clubs and this new scheme gave them the chance to carry on playing football while continuing their education. They got the best of both worlds – time to study academically while also training as full-time footballers.

At best, it was envisaged that a handful might move into the professional game, (which has proved to be the case), while others could earn a part-time income playing non-League football. The rest might simply enjoy the experience – and either carry on in academia or pursue a career in another area.

Through the scheme's success Cirencester Town were able to furnish their first team with home-grown players without having to pay out transfer fees, and they consequently nudged up the English football pyramid from the Hellenic League (level nine) up to the British Gas Business (BGB) Southern Premier League (level seven), though in 2007-08 they dropped back into the BGB South and West Division (level eight) – four leagues beneath the Football League. Cirencester College generated positive PR and improved its sporting reputation by stealing a march on rival sports colleges and consequently hoovered up British Universities and Sports Association trophies.

It was done because it was doable, as long as the college and the club could justify the funding and both parties were committed to making it work.

They called it the Cirencester Town Academy – for that is how they literally perceived it to be: academically oriented. It also seemed to suit the spirit of the era when the word 'academy' was coming back into vogue and, in US collegiate terms, was par for the course. It was truly a win-win situation.

But then, in 1999, the FA blundered in, claiming bizarrely that, in football at least, the word 'academy' suddenly belonged to them and no one else could use it for fear of confusion. It's worth remembering that at this point the FA was still an old-fashioned organisation, issuing dictums from its oak-panelled offices in Lancaster Gate. Today, football's governing body, which relocated to its slick chrome and pine offices in Soho Square in 2000 when Adam Crozier was appointed as chief executive, would surely have spotted this as a PR own goal. A large organisation pushing a little guy around, mainly for getting there first or for using a word they didn't like (a word, incidentally, that Cirencester had lodged at Companies House).

So why were the FA so upset with little ol' Cirencester and their academy? Why did the governing body try to use its might to sweep aside this small club? The answer is that it reflected the FA's aspirations at the time, because a bigger game was in play.

In 1997 Howard Wilkinson had swept into the chair as head of the FA's technical department. The former Leeds manager (and still, incidentally, the last English manager to win the Football League Division One championship – today's Premier League title) had been sacked by the Yorkshire club in September 1996, but in his new role immediately set to work with his plan to reshape youth development in England.

Bluff, austere, but always personable, Wilkinson did not match the time-honoured image of your traditional FA man. A former player, he had managed three professional clubs in the top flight and was seen as a friend of the professional game. His predecessor, Charles Hughes, had been schooled in a different tradition with a background in amateur football and education. He'd briefly gained notoriety with the launch of his book, *The Winning Formula: Soccer Skill and Tactics*, a coaching text which appeared to advocate the long-ball game, which included gathering its proof from analysis of every World Cup final. One of the teams he had rounded upon was the 1970s Brazil side for making too many passes.

Hughes' approved methods seemed outdated – harking back to the methodology of Wing Commander Charles Reep, who, in the 1950s, had noted that most goals were scored from moves involving three passes or less. Whereas Reep could point to the highly successful free-scoring Wolves team in his era as a positive example of this theory (Wolves played with two wingers so the ball was swept out to them, then crossed forwards to score), Hughes' assertion in the 1990s was linked, erroneously, to critics of long ball protagonists such as Wimbledon's 'Crazy Gang' – a team noted for their physical style of play.

The press corps rounded on Hughes. 'Charles expressed his views rather too robustly,' a former colleague of his said.

By contrast, Wilkinson, although not readily recognised as a smooth operator and uneasy about the sort of charm offensive and schmoozing that is sometimes required to get policy driven through committees, is, as one of his colleagues put it, 'a skilled politician'.

Although not averse to barking short, sharp single-syllable messages at players, Wilkinson is known as a long-term, developmental thinker – a rare breed among football managers. He understood the professional game, but had credence among the school and FA regional network too – yes, Howard would do.

He set to work immediately by reshaping elite youth development at professional clubs, laying out his plans in the document called *A Charter for Quality*. It called for a dramatic shake-up of youth development. It was envisaged that well-heeled Premier League clubs would run their own academies, while their poorer relations in the Football League's three divisions would opt for cheaper, more cheerful versions called centres of excellence, all run under licence of the FA. It was a commendable piece of work – a thorough revamp of youth development. Written within Wilkinson's first hundred days in office, *A Charter for Quality* plotted a new course for the development of home-grown players.

The FA was proud to be introducing the word 'academy' into the lexicon of football. In Britain, the word was readily associated with elitist education in a particular field – for example in fine art or culture – or in military training, possibly at red brick universities and sometimes bundled with royal patronage. The word had also sprung back into fashion through the New Labour government's attempts at transforming previously failing schools by renovating them with a blend of public and private investment, the Private Finance Initiative (PFI), where the new 'academies' focused on a particular area of expertise. The first to open was a business academy in Bexley, Kent, in 2002.

In other cultures the word has different connotations. In many continental European countries it has a linguistic link to the ancient Greek definition of 'gymnasium', literally 'a place to prepare', so therefore, theoretically less than a college of learning, for instance, than a preparatory school. In France, academies are councils that supervise education in regions. It isn't necessarily, therefore, always an elitist word.

The actual origin of the word derives from ancient Greece; *Akademeia*, from *Akademos,* is the name of the garden where Plato taught his students from around the time of 387 BC.

Despite the lofty ideals of the *Charter for Quality*, the idea of claiming the word 'academy' as the FA's own seemed risible because, back in the 1990s, the educational track record of the game's professional clubs' youth trainees was lamentable. Players took day release vocational or BTEC courses at local colleges, but the failure rate was high. The clubs didn't always encourage their players' participation in their college work. 'Some clubs always produced high levels of support but many saw their major function to produce footballers,' recalls former Huddersfield Town and Sheffield Wednesday chief executive Alan Sykes, who now runs League Football Education (LFE), the newly formed charity that oversees education programmes at Football League clubs. 'There were exceptions – but there were people who thought, "So what?" if a player missed college. "He's here to learn to be a footballer".' At 18, many trainees found themselves high and dry – they weren't offered a professional contract by their club and had very little, if anything, academically or vocationally, to fall back on.

The folks running the Cirencester Academy weren't daft. They had lodged their business name with Companies House – the FA couldn't make them change it. The college wasn't going to be pushed around either. The college's principal, Nigel Robbins, awarded an OBE for his services to education in 2005, was an academic man through and through, right down to his corduroy jacket. 'The idea that the FA thought they could monopolise this word 'academy' seemed farcical really, because it is a common word that has been in use since the time of the ancient Greeks,' smiled Robbins. 'If it had come to legal action they would have lost hands down. I don't think there is any question about that. But we were given some pretty clear instructions by the FA, which is barmy really. At the time, it was quite scary, so we subtly dropped the word from our literature.'

Staff at the Cirencester Academy were dismayed at the action of the FA. Their establishment had been designed and set up to meet a need within the football industry. 'When I first heard the suggestion to set up the academy, I jumped at the chance,' said Robbins. 'We felt that, together with the club, we were coming up with a solution to a problem that was affecting lots of young footballers, who, having been taken on by professional clubs as YTS trainees, were getting a pretty poor education in comparison to their peers who had stayed in sixth-form education.'

And the new academy was good at what it were doing. Under the careful tutelage of former Swindon Town player Dave Hockaday, their first academy director, they won the English Schools FA Under-18 Cup four times in five years. When they played professional clubs in the South-West Youth League they more than held their own. The idea of this as a hicks-in-the-sticks project out to belittle the whole of FA's academy structure was untrue. In its own terms Cirencester was very successful. Although the academy actually ran out of funds at one point, Robbins found money within the college's budget to cover the costs of the academy staff's wages.

Several players that passed through its hands were signed by League clubs, others moved on to Conference clubs, and several progressed into Cirencester Town's first team. Former Cirencester Academy pupils include Matt Green, who joined Swansea City, and Stuart Nelson, who is at Norwich City.

Of the players at the Cirencester Academy back in 2001, many had bad experiences during their time at supposed superior professional clubs. Some had seen teams from their age groups disbanded for financial reasons. Others, like Jeremy Flowerdew, had been ousted from his club's centre of excellence because he'd had a growth spurt at 16, and, as anyone who knows the slightest thing about such matters will appreciate, boys struggle physically to adjust at this awkward time in their development. However, his club's first-team manager had a homespun ethos of expecting his youth team players to be ready for first-team action at 17.

But there was even worse news for the FA. It seemed that Cirencester's model was being replicated by other clubs and colleges around the country. 'Initially it had been us, but there was an appetite to roll this out among other colleges,' recalled Nigel Robbins. 'We held a couple of conferences about college football academies and it was clear that many other colleges wanted to run their own football courses. So it grew.'

A league, the Programme for Academic and Sporting Excellence (PASE), was formed for participating non-League clubs. Cirencester aside, the FA were able to prevent the remaining college football schemes from being called academies. Flushed with success, the FA moved on to the word 'excellence' – the term now used in the new elite youth set-ups; academies were at Premier League clubs and centres of excellence were in the lower leagues.

The FA decided to flex its muscles again by refusing to support a grant application that the PASE, organised by Bedford College at the time, had filed with Sport England's Sportsmatch fund (a nifty scheme that allows the government to effectively double the money for a worthy sports project by matching the sum a commercial partner is prepared to offer in order to help the project grow). With the support of the Nationwide Building Society and Sports Minister at-the-time Kate Hoey, the PASE was confident it would get their funding if the FA supported its application. But the FA refused.

This seems quite remarkable. Here was a scheme designed to help the development of young footballers (maybe not quite the elite in the new formed academies or centres of excellence, but not far behind) whose primary funding was coming from education, but who saw a chance to bring fresh revenue into the sport. Without it, PASE was stymied. Its project manager at the time, Teresa Frith, was frustrated and disappointed, 'The FA didn't feel able to support the application for Sportsmatch funding, which we found very upsetting.'

When asked for his opinion on the matter at the time Howard Wilkinson wrote, 'the *Charter for Quality* had at its basis the development of elite young footballers and it is unrealistic and unfair to expect non-League clubs to make a contribution to this area.' His assistant, Robin Russell, was despatched to tell a meeting of angry Conference chairmen that he didn't believe non-League clubs would ever produce future England players. This did not go down well.

At the time the upper echelon of the game was littered with players whose careers had started in non-League football including three recent captains of British national teams, Stuart Pearce (England),

Vinnie Jones (Wales) and Andy Townsend (Republic of Ireland), while the likes of Kevin Phillips, Les Ferdinand and Lee Hughes were hammering in goals for fun in the Premier and Football League. England's 1990 World Cup team contained several ex-non-League players including Pearce, Chris Waddle, Paul Parker and Steve Bull.

Oh, and Marc Richards, an England Under-18 youth international, had just moved from Hednesford Town, at the time a Vauxhall Conference club, to Premier League Blackburn Rovers. Any idea that the non-League game would simply wither away disinterested in unearthing its own rough diamonds and that none – none at all – would float upwards into the professional game seemed unlikely.

Eventually the FA backtracked, and supported PASE, though not in time to secure the funding it required. Ironically, the FA now recognises college sport and pumps substantial funds into it. So why was it in such a tizz about the workings of a small non-League club 93 miles from Lancaster Gate?

It was all about control. Earlier in the decade the FA had controversially given its blessing (and lent its name) to a breakaway league of the country's top clubs, including the likes of Manchester United, Arsenal and Liverpool, but also less obvious perennial giants of the game as QPR, Wimbledon and Oldham. The new league's motto was, 'Sod the rest, let's share the TV loot'. Or more politely, 'One of the reasons the Premier League was formed was that the big clubs didn't want to be held back by the smaller clubs,' says Premier League general secretary, Mike Foster. 'The voting structure of the old 92 club Football League clubs meant the smaller ones could stop the larger clubs from forging ahead. But the gap between the Manchester United's and the Rochdale's was huge. There was frustration among the big clubs, who felt they were being held back.'

The top clubs got their desired result following the creation of the Premier League. They found a new supply of money – and therefore power – from satellite TV, and BSkyB in particular – which they did not have to share with the lower league clubs, a situation so appalling for the future development of football in England that they, along with the FA and the government via the Football Foundation, were later levied to provide a small slice of their income to the grass roots of the game.

Fuelled by successive TV deals the Premier League has been a huge success story and casts its mighty shadow over the rest of the English game. The Premier League's annual turnover in 2007 was £954 million, dwarfing the FA's turnover of £238 million for the same period by £716 million. Along with this financial muscle has come power, with places for representatives of the top clubs on any number of the FA's committees. The committee controlling youth development, for example, was the Technical Control Board chaired, at stages, by Premier League chairmen to approve and oversee Wilkinson's plans.

What the professional clubs wanted was the chance to develop their own players in-house from an early age rather than risk losing them to rival clubs. Some said they wanted to roll out the experience of a different educational institute – the FA National School at Lilleshall.

The top clubs also complained that they were fed up with losing players to the England team and age, representative sides. In 1997, in *A Charter for Quality*, they got the shake-up they wanted – delivered by Wilkinson and the FA itself.

The Cirencester story therefore seemed to be making sense. When questioned about the FA's seemingly intransigent stance over Cirencester, Robin Russell sent me a copy of the *Charter for Quality*. 'It will answer all your questions,' he said.

A closer examination of the charter is illuminating. Although it isn't particularly well presented, with just a few basic graphs and no pictures, it does, rather like its author, get straight to the point and spells out its aims with admirable clarity.

Subtitled 'Football Education for Young Footballers', Wilkinson's plan to develop the country's elite footballers – 'the top 1 per cent' – calls for many things based on a unified approach. Above all it stresses the overriding requirement 'to put the needs of the player first'. The second buzzword is quality – in particular 'quality control' and a 'quality audit', described as 'critical', and the need to 'monitor, review and evaluate the operation of the centres of excellence and football academies'.

The author acknowledged that clubs wanted to invest more time and resources in developing young players – the same access, indeed, as the FA National School was having – to coach youngsters up to four times a week. He said the FA was 'delighted' that clubs wished to invest more time and money into the development of young players.

His concerns about overplay and the existing 'fragmented and unstructured match programme' are noted, and Wilkinson believed it was 'reasonable' to allow more access to clubs who were prepared 'to provide the best possible coaches in the best possible facilities.'

But – and this is a key point – Wilkinson adds, 'this access should only be available to those clubs who ... appreciably increase and improve their quality of provision'.

In bold letters, Wilkinson outlined a number of 'fundamental' points in shaping the players' match programme. This includes the involvement of parents, his/her school, and the employment of education and welfare officers. He stressed the point that, 'I would hope that schools would continue to play a central part in the provision of quality for our young boys and girls'.

Significantly, Wilkinson added his desire to see the construction of a National Football Centre to accompany the charter (something that still hasn't happened), and finally he warned that football 'can suffer from the perils of fragmentation,' but he is 'delighted' to propose recommendations that emphasise 'quality and ... unity'.

But Wilkinson must have written those words in hope rather than expectation. What sort of 'unity' did he expect? When have football clubs ever shown a united front when it comes to competing for the signatures of the best players, whether they are young boys or seasoned professionals? Where was this all-for-one-and-one-for-all spirit when the FA Premier League was formed just four years earlier?

It is hard to imagine that such fine thoughts would have captured the attention of many club directors, who will have thumbed straight to Section G and read it with glee, in particular items 4 and 5: the criteria to operate either a football academy or to run a centre of excellence.

The first rule was that academies *must* operate at every age level from under 9 years old through to 21, (for centres of excellence this was optional although they had to cover the 14–16-year-old age brackets). This was remarkable. It shifted the previous age limit from 14 years old to under 9 years old, crossing the boundary into primary school-age children.

More significantly, the players were not just offered training opportunities. They had to be 'registered' – in other words they would be contracted, and therefore tied, to the clubs. Both academies and centres of excellence were allowed to sign a maximum of 40 boys in each age band between the ages of nine and 12, 30 between 13 and 14 and 20 per age group above that. This was the recruitment of children on a massive scale, club-by-club.

Boys aged below 9 and up to 12 were to sign for one year at a time; at 12, 14 and 16 they could sign for two years (or four years at 12, if they wished). But let's make it clear (as we will see): this did not compel the club to provide one or two years of professional football club coaching, rather it only tied the boy to the club. It hung in the club's favour. They could say 'ta-ra' to you whenever they liked, but the player coulndn't leave them until their contract was up.

But there's more. Clubs were also granted permission to set up 'satellite' centres away from the main academy grounds, which, although not allowing them to increase the overall number of players in their academy, would enable them to sift through more players who could go 'on trial' for a maximum of six weeks at each club. After that a club would have to decide whether it wanted to sign a player or not.

This must have read like manna from heaven to the clubs. Of course, there were strings attached. They could only sign boys who lived within a maximum travel time of the academy they were attending. For boys under 13 years of age this is one hour, for those between 13 and 16, it is an hour-and-a-half, and this is not applicable to full-time scholars or apprentices over 16 years old who can come from where they like in the world (and often do these days!).

However, since the charter's publication the satellite centres have expanded (and clubs can run ten development centres to prepare under nine year olds for the academy or centre of excellence) to gain maximum reach and clubs will frequently stretch them across their patch. Aston Villa, for example, set their satellite centre out as far west as Hereford, and east towards Leicester. Southampton were able to sign a Cardiff-based player, Gareth Bale, by having a satellite centre in Bath – just within the one-hour travel time from Cardiff, even though the distance between Southampton to Cardiff is 137 miles, so clearly out of reach within one hour or one-and-a-half hours.

In its defence the travel rule was just one of a number of child protection measures that Wilkinson introduced and which was also designed, it must be said, to allow smaller clubs a chance to develop local players. However, to some Premier League clubs who want to sign the best players regardless of where they live, the travel rule, in combination with the geographical limits on where they could open their satellite centres, was a contentious issue. They didn't readily accept it either, and despite the best efforts of inspectors, some clubs found ways and means to circumvent the rules.

In terms of coaching, Wilkinson also demanded that clubs should provide a minimum number of hours coaching time per week: for 9 to 11 year olds, not less than three hours over two sessions per week, for 12 to 16 year olds not less than five hours, and for 17 to 21 year olds not less than 12 hours. All boys under 16 should have the chance to play between 24 and 30 matches a season.

Clubs were compelled to have minimum coach-to-player ratios (two coaches to 20 players) and employ specialist goalkeeping coaches for 50 per cent of the technical sessions. Academies were required to have appropriately qualified staff, although in a centre for excellence assistant coaches could be employed while working towards their required qualifications. This, it should be noted, was recommended to cover the transitional period during which clubs moved from their old youth set-ups to the new centres. When Richard Lewis conducted his review in 2007, he was amazed to find that clubs were continuing to employ unqualified staff, who were only prepared to gear up for their job once they had secured it. All staff were also to be committed to 36 hours per year towards Continuous Professional Development (CPD) via in-service training.

The charter also required that each club had to employ appropriately qualified medical staff for training sessions and matches, and provide physiological assessment and feedback. They were required to appoint an education and welfare officer, whose role it is to liaise with players, parents and schools. 'The players' … academic potential must be catered for and not compromised,' warned Wilkinson.

Full-time over-16-year-old scholars must have a suitable education programme.

Wilkinson also laid out requirements for facilities – the rules differing considerably between those expected of a fully fledged academy (requiring at least three outdoor pitches and an indoor complex) and centres of excellence, which need only vague facilities (such as an 'appropriate size of coaching area' and 'adequate showers and bathing facilities'). Academies also needed a parents lounge and study areas for players. The charter included recommendations on the proposed make-up of inspection panels, a new set of coaching qualifications including the Pro Licence for top coaches (which Wilkinson steered through before leaving the FA in 2002).

Youth development coaches warmly welcomed the charter. 'For the first time we had a document that spelt out an integrated approach to the development of young players,' recalls Huw Jennings. 'It was a holistic approach that supported the needs of the player on and off the pitch.' Dave Parnaby, former manager of the England Under-15s and soon-to-be appointed director of the academy at Middlesbrough, thought it was, 'an excellent document that would take us forward as a nation'.

Sadly, Wilkinson's call for unity fell on deaf ears. 'This will work fine,' said one of the game's most experienced managers at one of the first meetings of newly appointed academy directors, 'Until one of you bastards crosses another'. The clubs were not interested in unity, they wanted to produce better players for themselves and set about interpreting the charter for their own ends.

Some clubs accepted the new regulations 'grudgingly', some failed to build the required new facilities. Others were even more cynical, revealing the central problem of handing so much power over to professional clubs. Logic tells you that if clubs can recruit children under nine years old, they must by definition, go hunting for younger ages – eight, seven, maybe even six. The reality is even worse than that with five and even four year olds being actively chased.

Another alarming effect of the charter is the number of boys now being trained by professional clubs. It spelled out that a mandatory requirement for academies was to have a team in each age band in order to gain and maintain a licence. So, 92 clubs, ten age groups with a minimum of 15 players in each group. That's 13,000 players! OK, knock off a few clubs who are moving in and out of the Football League or those falling on hard times – make that ten players per team and it is still about 10,000 boys. And that, today, is roughly how many boys are signed to academies or centres of excellence.

How many will get taken on at the end of their scholarship at 18 or 19 – a handful per club? The Football League estimates its member clubs have taken on 600 youth players in the past four years. Sounds good, but that is only eight per club – two, on average, per season. Not many.

And what chance do the eight and nine year olds stand of making it through the various levels? What about the welfare implications for the younger ones? What happens to those who fail? Boys whose hopes have been hoisted by attending these super duper centres? Lads who have been told, in order to boost their egos, that they are special and will make it? What happens when the dream dies?

Although Wilkinson's *Charter for Quality* was clearly going to make a massive and positive difference to youth development in England, it also put a heavy weight on the country's football clubs who were going to need to invest heavily in their training facilities – and an even greater seismic shift in the terms of the way they would need to handle the many and varied concerns of boys entering these new academies and centres of excellence.

CHAPTER 4

OPPORTUNITY KNOCKS

Only in his wildest dreams could Howard Wilkinson have imagined that the newfound vision of academies he laid out in the *Charter for Quality* would come to such stunning fruition at Aston Villa's opulent training ground at Bodymoor Heath in the Warwickshire countryside. The facilities here would turn the head of any aspiring young footballer. A distant golf club thwack away from the Belfry, scene of many of golf's Ryder Cup dramas, Villa's academy players share the recently expanded £13-million complex with the senior squad.

The club now has 12 neatly manicured outdoor pitches here, eight for the academy, four for the senior teams, most which you pass on the long drive to their indoor complex. This resembles a college in the sticks more than a set of football club changing rooms. The indoor centre has the obligatory third generation (3G) indoor training arena, lounge and viewing areas for parents, and a vast array of changing rooms – with each age group of players having their own set of facilities.

Villa are not alone. Only a jaundiced eye would fail to see that Premier League clubs have been true to their word – most have invested heavily in their academies, which deliver both fantastic facilities and the staff required to operate them. According to Richard Lewis's *Review of Young Player Development in Professional Football* (or the *Lewis Report*) into young player development of 2007, English football is spending 3.3 per cent of its income on youth development, which, unlike many other aspects of the top end of football's distorted spending, is broadly in line with most other industries investment in research and development.

Situated 16 miles from Villa Park, the club's home in inner city Aston, Bodymoor Heath is testimony to the value of being a regular member of the Premier League since its inception in 1993. Villa are snugly nestled among the league's hierarchy and under American owner Randy Lerner's shrewd, but laid back, boardroom management, and first-team manager Martin O'Neill's more effervescent approach, Villa seem on the verge of muscling into the Premier League's so-called 'Big Four' – Manchester United, Chelsea, Arsenal and Liverpool.

Youth development has played a big part in Villa's recent success. They were crowned National Academy League Under-18 champions in 2007-08, and many of their current first-team squad came through the academy, most notably pacy England Under-21 forward Gabby Agbonlahor, but also Nathan Delfouneso, Craig Gardner and Isaiah Osbourne. Ciaran Clarke, Nathan Baker, Irish duo Stephen O'Halloran and Barry Bannan, and Australian Chris Herd are also waiting in the wings.

Villa's patient approach to youth development has been shaped by a stable team led by academy director Brian Jones, along with his assistant Steve Burns, education and welfare officer Paul Brackwell – all ex-schoolteachers – and coaches Tony McAndrew and Gordon Cowans, both former players. All have been here since the academy opened in 1998.

Villa's academy alumni include Gary Cahill, Liam Ridgewell, Steve Davis, Stephen Cooke, Peter Whittingham, Rob Edwards, and brothers Luke and Stefan Moore, all players who have now moved on. But Villa had a decent track in finding their own stars way before the academy system began. Club captain Gareth Barry signed as a 16-year-old trainee from Brighton and Hove Albion, and has been polished into a senior England international. Lee Hendry and Darius Vassell are other fairly recent home-grown England players – and, further back, Jones also developed the likes of Mark Walters and Tony Daley in the pre-academy era.

Jones has seen youth development undergo a huge transformation since he joined Villa as a part-time youth coach in 1977, in the primitive days when they trained on the car park. Other than a couple of short spells elsewhere (he reckons he didn't 'see eye-to-eye' with a couple of managers), he has worked for the club full time since 1980, and has been academy director since their facility first opened its doors.

Villa estimate one-third of the players offered scholarship forms at 16 have signed contracts as 18 year olds – that is almost twice the average of most clubs. This is an impressive figure, and proof positive that, academy-wise, they are on the right track. The club spends £2 million a year running the academy – which is the Premier League average. 'We estimate Premier League clubs invest about £40 million in their academies,' Premier League general secretary, Mike Foster told me. 'We think it has gone very well. We are proud of what has been accomplished and the way clubs have invested in their academies. The facilities at our major clubs are world class.'

Huw Jennings, the Premier League's former head of youth development, says the quality of players being produced by academies is better than ever. 'Without question,' said Jennings. 'If you speak to most youth developers the skill levels, the ball mastery, balance and flexibility of our young players is better than it has ever been.'

However, what is missing is opportunity. 'We must create an environment where talent can meet opportunity. Clubs need to have an integrated approach. It makes financial sense. The player affinity is greater and you save on buying in players,' he commented.

This is precisely what they do at Middlesbrough FC, a team that is also able to tell an academy success story. There was a palpable sense of excitement at their Rockcliffe Park academy on a Friday afternoon in January 2009. First-team manager Gareth Southgate had announced his team for the following day and 19-year-old defender Josh Walker had been selected to make his first Premier League start in a north-east derby against Sunderland.

Every boy's dream, or what? Walker is the latest in a line of players to roll off the Rockcliffe Park production line and academy manager Dave Parnaby can barely hide his delight. 'It's fantastic for him,' beams Parnaby. 'He's only 19 but he seems to have been around forever'. That's because the former England Under-16, Under-17 and

Under-18 captain has been in Middlesbrough academies for 10 years. In fact, since the academy first opened in August 1998.

'That is how long it takes to get a player out on to the first-team pitch,' says Parnaby. 'You are judged by how many players you get through to your first team. It requires patience, so I sympathise with those people in my position at other clubs who get asked why did we lose games at this age or that age level. We never get asked that here, so we're lucky. If the chairman, chief executive and first-team manager don't understand and appreciate that, then it is tough.'

Parnaby, a quietly spoken Teessider, has had some success at Boro, and in 2004 his youth team lifted the FA Youth Cup. But he isn't in it for personal glory – more to give chances to boys like full internationals Stewart Downing, Chris Brunt, James Morrison, and England Under-21 players Andrew Taylor and Lee Cattermole.

Rockcliffe Park is state-of-the-art, with an annual budget for the academy of roughly £1 million. But that doesn't tell the whole story. 'We work hard at creating the right culture. That, with good talent identification, coaching and opportunity means we can produce players from a relatively local area,' Parnaby explained. 'We live in an area where local football is vibrant and participation in junior football is high.'

Boro recruit much of their talent from local leagues – principally the Teesside Junior Alliance – one of the largest junior leagues in Europe. The club has a healthy relationship with the league, something that Parnaby has worked hard at developing. It isn't just on the take for players – but puts something back in terms of coaching, resources and contact, which isn't always the case with professional clubs and their local junior football network.

The management brief, handed down from chairman Steve Gibson, is to give opportunities to the people of Teesside. Gibson is a man with an acute sense of local pride. A Labour councillor at the age of 21, he is now a self-made, multi-millionaire – listed 644th on the 2008 *Sunday Times* Rich List and worth an estimated £112 million.

The academy recruits players predominantly from within a 35-mile radius. Incredibly, on the final day of the 2005-06 season, former Boro manager Steve McClaren fielded an all-English team (not just the 11 players who started, but also the five substitutes) who were all born, with the exception of striker Malcolm Christie, within a 30-minute drive of Middlesbrough.

'The fans are proud of the boys who do come through,' said Parnaby. 'Can we sustain it? That's the challenge. There is good youth development at a lot of clubs, but what is missing is opportunity. We are participating in the strongest league in the world. The challenge in youth development is greater because the bar for the players gets higher.'

However, as the *Meltdown* report revealed, the Premier League now has many more foreign players than English players, with the crossover happening a couple of years after the academy system clicked into gear. Sadly, the emerging talent has not reversed the trend. Across the board home-grown players are simply not getting the opportunity to progress to first-team football. During some weeks of the 2008-09 season, overseas players made up 75 per cent of the starting line-ups in Premier League matches. Along the way, there have been some equally depressing statistics.

FA figures for the 2001-02 season showed that no 17 or 18 year olds started matches in the Premiership. In the 2003-04 season, just 60 under-23 players had played in the Premier League all season – a measly 103 of the Premier League's 900 footballers of all ages were brought through by the clubs for which they were playing.

It is estimated that for every six players who sign professional contracts after leaving an academy aged 18, five are out of the game by the time they're 21. When the Football League say that 600 players have signed professional contracts at their member clubs in the past four years, in reality it means, on average, only 60 stay in the game longer than three years.

There are many reasons for this: the Bosman ruling, transfer windows and freedom of contract have seen the domestic transfer market dry up, and the age-old process of smaller clubs selling upwards has reversed. The top clubs have realised that if they get the talent in as early as possible they can avoid paying transfer fees when players become professionals. The result is that there are fewer players moving between the lower leagues and the Premier League. However, because they can't find openings at their clubs, Premier League academy players are being loaned out to get experience, or sold on so that clubs can recoup some of their expenditure. The stakes are now so high, and not just for lucrative Champions League or UEFA Cup places, but for prize money for each Premier League spot, that managers have few opportunities to experiment.

Agents are also keen to dump DVDs of their clients in action on to first-team managers' desks, whose jobs themselves are increasingly on the line. Since the academies were introduced the average period a manager stays in charge of an English Premier or Football League club has dipped below 18 months. As one high profile manager said, 'What do you do if you have a problem? Try a raw, young player or bring in an experienced international with maybe 30 caps under his belt that an agent can promise to deliver to your training ground within a week?' It is a no-brainer for most gaffers, but it is making life tougher in the academies. In a strange schizophrenia, top clubs are pouring unprecedented sums into youth development, but offering fewer openings to the players who emerge.

By January 2009 the Premier League had hosted eight under-19 debutants (compared with eight in the whole of the previous season). Premier League general secretary Mike Foster portrayed this modest statistic as some sort of triumph. But only 66 academy players had appeared on club team sheets (including substitutes – and, remember, clubs can now field seven of them) up to that point in the season.

The reality is even grimmer than that, 'You have to be careful with definitions of home-grown players,' he warned. 'If you take UEFA's definition of "home-grown" (any player who was recruited under the age of 19 has been at the club for three or more years), the Premier League team with the most home-grown players is Arsenal who bring players into their academy at 16 from anywhere in the world. If you are talking about English players who have come through the entire system it is a different set of data.'

For every Villa or Middlesbrough there are clubs with hardly any locally developed players in their first-team squad. Liverpool for example, have just two in their 41-player, first-team squad – Steven Gerrard and Jamie Carragher – both produced before the academy era. Incredibly, Liverpool had 15 players being loaned out at the time this book went to press, ten of them to Football League clubs, who, no longer able to dig themselves out of any financial holes they may slip into, cannot sell their prized assets as a way out of their troubles. The top clubs, having searched younger than ever for players, now snap up all of the best players while they are at school. The cheaper alternative for small clubs is to supplement their squads by bringing players in on loan.

Howard Wilkinson believes this can be a good thing. 'Alex Ferguson will tell you that David Beckham needed the time he spent on loan to Preston before he reached Manchester United's first team to get some experience.' Indeed the architect of the academy system, who is disappointed with the lack of openings being offered to English talent, is calling for better links between bigger and smaller clubs, so that opportunities can be formalised.

It isn't just fringe players, but promising international players who are also being loaned out. Stuart Pearce, England's Under-21 manager, now watches more matches in the Championship than he does in the Premier League, as that is where most of his recruits play their football. Being an England prospect is no longer a guarantee that you will play in a top Premier League club's first team.

This is a problem for English football. 'Any analysis of international football will tell you that the successful countries who win major competitions do so with players competing in the top five clubs in the top five European leagues,' said Wilkinson.

So the openings, more than ten years after the academy system began, are slimmer than ever. The knock-on effect is that, in order to develop world-class players, clubs are desperate to recruit the best. 'First and foremost your talent identification has to be right,' says Dave Parnaby. 'Your scouting network has to be in good order. Your raw material has to be good.' Brian Jones at Aston Villa added, 'If you don't get the recruitment right the rest is a waste of time.'

The battle to sign the best youngsters has intensified into little more than an undignified scramble, with clubs increasingly searching for younger and younger players. As we have already seen this has been spurred on partly by the academy rules which demand – not recommend, but demand – that any club seeking to run an academy has to field a full range of teams from under nine year olds upwards.

To sign players at under-nine level you have to look for younger boys or risk losing them to fellow clubs. Wilkinson expected only established Premier League clubs to want to run academies, believing most Football League clubs would opt for cheaper and easier-to-run centres of excellence. But in the event 38 academy applications thudded onto the FA's doorstep. Instead of restricting the numbers to ensure quality, all of the applications were accepted when the initial licences were doled out at the start of the 2001-02 season. To compound their problem the FA then handed responsibility for the monitoring of standards to the respective leagues – the Premier League and Football League. In other words, the leagues inspect their own member clubs. This was a decision that would come back to haunt them.

Today there are 40 academies and 48 centres of excellence or, to put it another way, 88 professional clubs chasing pre-teen junior school-age boys at a time when the odds of these players breaking through is narrower than ever – each player is estimated to have a one in a hundred chance of signing a professional contract at age 18.

The clubs may have their education and welfare officers in post – but how much caution are clubs really exercising when recruiting them? 'My son plays in a junior football league in Warrington that is heavily scouted by several different north-west clubs,' said Andy Burnham. 'He was invited to train with a club at seven years old.'

The minister is lucky. Elsewhere the age is much lower. A few years ago, one Premier League club actually employed three full-time coaches to scour their patch for players as young as five. Some say it has descended even lower.

'You get scouts signing players when they are four years old,' said Rick Fenoglio, senior lecturer and researcher in Exercise and Sport Science at Manchester Metropolitan University. 'I can give you the name of places locally, where during the Easter and summer holidays and one night a week four and five year olds are being courted by clubs affiliated to Premiership and Championship clubs.'

There is a story of a prominent Premier League club coaching a boy who, when he bent down, was clearly wearing a nappy underneath his shorts. Not yet able to control his bowel movements but, hey, what does that matter if he can trap a football?

Fenoglio describes the search of talent as 'an interesting socio-logical phenomenon'. Fair enough, but why are they doing it? 'Competition and money,' said Fenoglio. 'Professional clubs want to develop good players so they can play for their first team, win games or they can sell them at a profit. That is what drives the industry. The offshoot is that we have a dream machine that thousands of boys are working towards. The problem is only 1 per cent of them make it and often it comes at the expense of their education, their social life and keeping their passion for the game alive. You have to ask whether academy coaches are the best people to look after the welfare, education and football development of such young boys.'

So how does the game justify chasing after boys who have barely kicked a ball in anger let alone developed a love for the game or sport in general? Mike Foster at the Premier League doesn't see a problem with clubs coaching such young boys, 'Not as long as it is handled correctly. Recruitment is a key part of youth development. Clubs are very active in their communities and if they identify talented young-sters at that age and put them into a slightly different environment I don't see that that should be a problem.'

When asked about the aims of the *Charter for Quality*, Howard Wilkinson always stresses that the needs of the player must come first. He acknowledges the internationally recognised criteria that it takes an estimated 10,000 hours of quality training time to develop an elite, winning sportsman – a calculation Sport England is currently calling 'Pitch to Podium'. The trouble is that footballers are getting nowhere near that amount of practice – which is why clubs want to develop them as young as possible.

'Practice time is a problem,' said Wilkinson. 'If you take a player between the ages of eight and 21 and divide those 10,000 hours by 13 years, and then by the number of weeks in a year and hours in a week – not including weekend matches and holidays – you can see that English players are not getting anywhere near the required amount of practice. What we need is imaginative, creative thinking between clubs, schools, local authorities, parents and community involvement to find the time for young footballers to get the practice time they need.'

Many people argue that English footballers need to spend the same amount of time that continental players spend with their clubs. Dave Richardson, a former school sports teacher who coached at Aston Villa (alongside Brian Jones) and Leicester City before becoming the Premier League's head of youth development, is aware of the apparent skills gap between young English and young continental players. He explained it by saying, 'The reason the continentals are technically better than us is because they get their players earlier and they don't have the inhibitions or the prohibitions that were around us with schools football. The leading continental countries have access to children from a very early age, and unlimited coaching time with them. It is finding the right age that children soak up information. That is what we are trying to do. It's recognised in educational circles that the golden ages of learning are from about eight or nine through to about 12 or 13 where your body and brain are like a sponge – that's the best time to take things in.'

But does that have to take place at a professional football academy? 'It is true that there is a certain amount of time people have to spend doing deliberate practice,' conceded Rick Fenoglio. 'There has been good research to say for a boy or girl to become an elite performer – whether it is music, drama, sport or anything – they have to actively work on their skills. That works out to be roughly 10,000 hours.

'But as good as many academy coaches may be there is no scientific evidence to prove that the idea that getting into formalised structures is the best way to develop them.' Fenoglio reckons it is down to more basic things – like sheer practice. 'If you add up the time players can spend playing football in academies they cannot get remotely anywhere near that amount of time. It is pointless to even think that you can. The number one factor by a long way that determines if someone is going to be a good footballer is the amount of time they actually spend engaged with the football, the amount of time they have a ball at their feet.

'People see children attending academies and think they are playing lots of football and developing, but there has been lots of time and motion analysis done on this and it is a lot less than people think. Kids would be better playing more informal soccer, playing on their own terms, having fun.'

This is a view shared by Sir Trevor Brooking, who, since he joined the FA as director of football development in December 2003, has been on a crusade to get better skills coaching for players aged between five and 11. 'We have a nation of couch potatoes and kids who play on computers. They don't play street soccer or in open spaces anymore for a variety of reasons', he explained. 'The only way you can improve at football is to have contact time with the ball. That is the biggest problem we have to address in getting a broad base of players from the ages of 5 to 11 years old who develop the right skills.'

But while Brooking and Wilkinson would like to develop an integrated approach to youth development that involves parents, schools, junior grass roots clubs and professional clubs, and have worked on plans for the FA to train a team of coaches to deliver skills coaching among that broad base of children, professional clubs have ploughed ahead trying to snap up the best young players they see, however young they are and in spite of the risks of putting them off football by making it too serious too soon in their lives.

Even club academy directors are not sure why they coach such young players. Brian Jones says, 'Aston Villa spend a fortune looking at boys from six years old onwards. With the best will in the world, I wouldn't know if a six, seven or eight year old is going to play in the Premier League in 10 or 12 years time. It's ludicrous.'

So why do they do it? 'Clubs fear if they don't sign the little ones up as soon as they can they may well lose them,' says Jones. This view is supported by Huw Jennings, who at Southampton discovered Theo Walcott, Gareth Bale and Andrew Surman among others, before moving to become the Premier League's head of youth development between 2006 and 2008. 'There is a lot of fear in youth development, fear of not getting the player. In the professional football game we are always going to come down to registration as a form of ownership. It is difficult when clubs invest as much as they do to say that they then can't have commitment from the player to play for them. Registration is something I think needs looking at with the youngest age groups up to 12. Having a coaching registration where a boy can play freely in the local community and come to the club for coaching might be a healthy way forward.'

Sometimes the modus operandi to recruit players is sneaky. 'The clubs use their community programme to effectively scout the best players,' said Dave Woollaston, a Luton schoolteacher and regional English Schools FA council member. 'They offer some coaching and put them into the development squad – effectively a holding team – it is a way of expanding the numbers of lads they have tied to them without really having a full commitment to them. They cast the net far and wide and trawl as far as they can. And, a bit like the fisherman who throws his net into the sea, as long as he gets the fish he wants he doesn't care about the fish he throws back overboard.'

On the other side of the coin, Brian Jones at Aston Villa says, 'The counter argument is you are coaching more boys and making them better players. But psychologically, I think you are building up such great hopes so when you reach the stage to say, "I'm sorry you aren't good enough," it kills them. It finishes them off.'

In 2008, Andrea (not her real name), put her six-year-old son, Jack (also not his real name), to bed in tears. Nothing unusual, kids cry. But these were sobs of sheer despair. A few hours earlier he had been told that he hadn't survived 'the cull' by a Premier League football club.

Cull – what a charming word to use. Check it out. It literally means, 'to collect or select, to gather or pick out (from the rest)'. But its most common usage is in referring to the killing of surplus animals to control the population stock and breeding.

So what led to Jack being 'culled'? In essence he was offered some football training for a few months, he wasn't among the best in the group so he wasn't selected to carry on ... he was culled. So, this little boy, like thousands of others like him, became a victim of football's self-serving greed. Not good enough – now get out of the way. Next!

Jack had only just started learning the rudiments of the sport and had joined a local junior club when a Premier League club scout sidled up, said he liked what he had seen and would be in touch. He was six years old, as mum Andrea put it, a 'no-gap-between-the-socks-and-shorts, little titch.'

The wait was, she recalls 'interminable' for him. Eventually the call came and Jack was invited to coaching sessions during the Easter holidays. She wasn't sure he should go, but dangle that carrot in front of a six-year-old kid and it'll take a lot to talk him out of it. The clubs know what they are doing. They know their powers of persuasion in our culture, even for little kids. Kids of six know all about the major clubs, the top players and so on. So when a man in a club tracksuit says he likes what he sees in you and invites you to 'training' at the club academy, of course you want to go.

Andrea, a university lecturer and hardly the stereotypical 'pushy parent' that academy coaches often moan about, was surprised on her first visit to the academy: 'There were even younger ones there than him.' Although no forms were signed, this was clearly more than a bit of casual coaching. 'They were given the club kit to wear,' recalls Andrea, who said that Jack and the other boys had to pass through a series of levels to see if they would reach the next step. 'If you don't hear from us after that you won't be going forward,' they were told at the beginning of the training.

The sessions, held at the club's former training ground, carried on over the summer months. Although Jack's football appeared to improve – Andrea readily admits she wouldn't really know – she noticed other palpable changes in her son. He was anxious. The twice-weekly training sessions 'got to his head,' she said. She wanted to ease him out of going, but he was enjoying playing football and scoring lots of goals. Then she paused for thought, 'but then he might have been doing that just playing with mates'.

Other parents were in the same boat. What had 'got' to Jack's head was selection for the next step. 'There was always another hoop to jump through and it disturbed him.' He was playing under pressure to perform, always being tested, and he didn't like it. There seemed to him to be so much at stake – a place in the club's proper academy. Retrospectively, Andrea acknowledges it was 'too much too soon'. But she says, like the other parents, she was skilfully strung along.

Eventually, with a cluster of other parents, she was told Jack had been culled – no one-to-one's or reasons offered – that was that, the training was over, for good. Andrea had to check with another parent that she'd heard the word 'culled' correctly.

She wanted to challenge the coach over the use of such awful language – but when you've got an upset little boy, what's the point?

Why prolong the agony? And anyway you just look like a sore loser – the proverbial pushy parent trying to question the coach's judgement.

'Looking back it was very businesslike,' says Andrea. 'The club didn't commit themselves to anything. The language was almost as if the boys were units to them, not people. There was no sense of connection. Their pulling power was all that mattered and they knew it.'

Jack went home. He didn't know what culled meant – but it probably sounded near enough like 'killed' to make him understand what had happened. His older sister, who had teased Jack about having lots of money, fast cars and a girlfriend, joked, 'I suppose we won't be rich and famous now after all'.

'I'm not ever going to be a footballer. I'm no good at it,' said Jack as his mum tried to comfort him in bed. What can a parent say? It's only someone's opinion? It's far too early in your life to say anything like that? They shouldn't even be looking at you, so young? What's important is who you are, not what someone says? Does it matter?

To hear that the man in the club tracksuit has 'culled' you – read it and weep, eh?

On the plus side when Andrea was interviewed, a year after the 'cull', she was able to report that Jack, then seven years old, had told her he was actually enjoying his football again … playing with his mates, 'without the pressure'. Good for him.

So what was the reaction to Jack's story from the leagues? 'You'll always have a range of quality, won't you?' commented the Premier League's Mike Foster. 'We are continuously trying to set the right standard. We have a booklet that sets out best practice. If our clubs are going to coach kids as young as five and six, then they have to do it responsibly.'

Graham Hawkins, the Football League's head of player development, was aghast the word 'culled' had been used but considered it a rare exception. 'You do hear of one or two complaints,' he said, 'but I don't think that is typical. They are not receiving any kind of PE at school so this is a form of PE, really.' What? Shouldn't football at six be about fun and not selectivity? 'It should be fun, replied Hawkins. 'We call that stage of development FUNdamental with the accent on the first three letters, and much of the practice isn't just about football, it's about agility, balance, coordination, speed (ABCs) and jumping.'

The reality is that there are thousands of 'Jacks' out there who are being told, week in, week out, that that they are – please let's not use the word 'culled' any longer, even though it may be part of football industry banter – not going to 'make it' as professional footballers. It is a horrendous thought: professional sports businesses – large, high-profile clubs with, in many cases, unfeasibly wealthy owners – are sifting through children, grubbing around for the best, enticing them in, and casually ditching the rest.

Brian Jones was appalled when he heard Jack's story. He rolled his eyes, 'It wouldn't happen if you employed people who knew how to work with children. When we sign a young player we make things very clear and we promise nothing. We choose our words carefully and say, 'you are invited to look at Aston Villa Football Club for six weeks during which time we will try and make you a better player. It is an experience and there's nothing guaranteed at the end of it.'

The players and parents or guardians who join Villa's academy have clear guidelines spelt out to them. 'Each July, we have a parents evening. We go through all the aspects of the academy, including the rulebook, which is handed to parents. It is fully explained and anything they don't understand we encourage them to ask.

'If we didn't have to sign these kiddies I could bring in 40 to 50 nine year olds each weekend, coach them, develop them and let them play for their junior clubs and do that for the next two or three years until they go to secondary school, then target the best players and sign them.'

It is to avoid the hideous disappointment that rejection is likely to engender that Jones and others would like to see the academy rules changed. 'I would prefer to see boys aged 9 to 11 invited once a week for coaching – not to play organised fixtures,' he explains, 'then go back to their Sunday clubs and schools to enjoy their football without any pressure. Then, when they are 12 years old, you can introduce organised games and start development work.'

Dave Parnaby agrees, 'It should start at 12. I have written to the FA and the Premier League. No one disagrees, but what is being done?

We should offer a coaching registration form for 9- to 11-year-old boys, then at 12, when they have naturally crossed over to secondary school level and can cope with the game a bit better, we invite them to coaching at the club.'

Instead some 10,000 boys a year are flooding into academies and centres of excellence – hoping against hope they might just become the next Beckham, Rooney or Walcott. It does happen, but only to the lucky 1 per cent.

CHAPTER 5

THE COMMITMENTS

Every school has a Clever Clogs who, to his peers, is an irritating natural at sport. At my junior school we had Gary Bowen – a boy two years below me, but able play for Stanley Road Junior School football and cricket teams when he was seven. He was exceptional at both. I remember us being skittled for just 24 runs in a cricket match and staring a heavy defeat in the face. Gary came on to bowl, on his debut, and took four wickets in his first over and seven overall. We tied the match, I think. That was the sort of kid Gary was at sport. Brilliant.

At Nunnery Wood Secondary School it was Stephen Wise – another all-round natural talent – captain of the school at football and cricket, and Head Boy, obviously. He had a beard at 14 and could punt goals in with effortless ease from the halfway line. Neither of these boys got anywhere close to sniffing a professional football contract and didn't even attract any interest at all as far as I knew. In fact, I only recall a few boys ever going on trial with professional football clubs during the whole of my schooldays. None of them made it. I used to wonder how good you have to be if Wise and Bowen didn't get a look in.

Dave Woollaston, a schoolteacher and English Schools FA council member, reckons my school was about average. Now, since the advent of football academies, he believes it is common for most schools to have between 10 and 15 pupils training with professional clubs. 'The blinkers come on,' said Woollaston, whose former pupils include West

Bromwich Albion defender Leon Barnett and another player featured in this book, Ricky Clarke. 'When a big club comes along and says we would like you to play for us, the boy believes he's made it. I don't think the clubs have to do too much selling. He sees the high life and the reports on TV and the lifestyles. Boys will be boys. They think they are going to be future millionaires. The parents also want to live the dream. But it only happens for 1 or 2 per cent. The other 98 or 99 per cent have their dreams burst.'

OK, so you're signed up – and the dream starts. What exactly is involved? Once the initial excitement of being taken on evaporates, there's lots of hard work and effort for sure – and that is only to get back and forth to training and matches. It is a big commitment for families, and with 10,000 players in the academy system it is causing its own little carbon footprint, with parents clocking up the miles, zigzagging across the country, driving to and from academies that are often tucked away in the remote countryside and unreachable by public transport.

Players are supposed to live within an hour-and-a-half's travel time of the academy or centre of excellence they are attending, so it's quite common for boys to travel for three hours each evening to play one-and-a-half hours of football. Yet it is a sacrifice that players and their parents are prepared to make, regardless of the statistical odds against them making it and the potential impact on the lives of the player, their mums and dads and other family members.

'Welcome to the madhouse,' says parent Adrian Craig cheerfully as I walk up the drive to his family's three-bedroom semi. He whistles his son Ryan in from outside, and explains how Coventry City's academy first spotted Ryan, then just eight years old, playing in a tournament in Torquay with a local junior club. He'd already been on trial at West Bromwich Albion, but was more impressed by Coventry's set up. 'They were the best club around for youth development when I was a kid,' recalls Adrian.

The Craigs live close to what used to be the giant Longbridge car factory in south Birmingham. The massive car plant, which finally closed when MG Rover went into administration in 2005 after years of gradual decline, is being dismantled brick by brick, leaving a huge expanse of derelict land on a site that once employed 25,000 people.

Even before the recession took hold work was hard to find around here. Although it isn't a particularly poor area, a small technology park built on a tiny part of the site cannot feed the local economy, in particular the component industries and shops, in the way that Longbridge once did. Mindful of this bleak industrial landscape, Adrian wants Ryan to make the best of his football skills. A talented district schools footballer, Ryan is also keen to progress in the sport.

Pulling a photograph of Ryan in Coventry's familiar sky blue kit down from the wall, Adrian recalls how proud he was when Ryan joined their academy. 'They were all over us and couldn't do enough for us,' said Adrian, who admits to being quizzical of Coventry's apparent need to have Ryan, a primary school boy at the time, training with them three nights a week and playing in weekend matches, which might have taken place anywhere in the country. After all, including travel time, it actually exceeded the hours Ryan spent at school. 'It was a big commitment, but we decided we were prepared to make the effort to give Ryan the best possible chance.'

For the next two years, Adrian, who works in Redditch, some seven miles from his home, nipped off early three times a week, losing money, so he could get home for 5 p.m. and grab a quick sandwich prepared by his wife, Michelle, to eat in the car en route to Coventry's training ground. 'I was lucky. My firm were good to me – not every parent could do this,' he noted. Training started at 6 p.m. 'It took about an hour to get there so it was always a bit of a rush,' recalls Adrian.

Coventry didn't seem particularly sympathetic to the travel difficulties of parents, 'they had a rule that if you were late for training twice in a week you wouldn't play at the weekend. I was travelling 30 miles so if I got stuck in traffic there was nothing I could do. If he was late, he was late, but to suggest it was the parents fault was wrong.'

Training usually finished at 7.30 most evenings. 'We would get home between 8.30 and 9 p.m. By the time he's had a shower and wound down it would be getting on for 10 p.m. That was late for a kid of his age.'

The Craigs fully accept that it was their choice to send Ryan to the academy, but from early on it was taking its toll, 'When I got home I was too tired to do my homework,' admitted Ryan. 'I was tired the next morning too. There didn't seem to be much free time.'

Football-wise, the constant rushing to and fro seemed to be worth-while. Ryan's football skills improved. But his age group were not achieving the results the club coaches insisted upon. 'They weren't having a good season and they were losing games,' explains Adrian. 'It stopped being fun,' says Ryan. 'You couldn't have a laugh with your mates. Sometimes they'd encourage you, but most of the time they just put you down. I thought it could have been better.'

Adrian started to have his doubts, 'I've known the children to come out of the changing rooms actually crying. You're talking nine- or ten-year-old kids. You don't do that to children.'

The Sunday matchday routine was particularly gruelling. 'It would take the whole day,' said Adrian. It began with a brisk 6 a.m. start with matches kicking-off at 11 a.m. 'You had to be there an hour early,' he recalled. 'For an away game we would have to drive to Coventry so Ryan could get the coach with the other players, then the parents would have to travel in their own cars.'

Coventry are not unique in adopting this rule – it is actually quite common – but is it is strange to imagine a half-empty team coach driv-ing to a faraway match followed by a flotilla of cars carrying the parents of nine- and ten-year-old kids prevented from travelling with their children.

At ten years old, Ryan was playing as far afield as Liverpool, Newcastle, Norwich and south London – all three to four-hour jour-neys. 'Charlton was the furthest,' said Adrian. 'Some kids would only get ten minutes worth of football and the parents had travelled for eight hours.' They were also expected to train during holiday times. 'They wanted him to go three days a week, other than two weeks you'd have off for your summer holidays,' said Adrian. 'I couldn't get him there in the week because of the times they wanted me to drop him off and collect him.' Eventually, the decision whether or not to carry on was taken out of their hands – it ended in tears.

Coventry is similar to many other clubs in terms of its youth devel-opment, but its academy is highly regarded in football circles in the

Midlands. The club has an understandable policy of refusing to comment on individual cases and preferred to issue a statement in relation to the issues raised in this chapter. It read, 'We have over 140 young players, the vast majority of whom all enjoy the experience they receive at Coventry City Football Club. It's impossible to keep every boy and parent completely happy. However, we always endeavour to do this.

'We give our young players an opportunity to train three nights per week (however, this is not compulsory) to accelerate their progress. There are strict restrictions on travelling distances to protect young players and parents are fully aware of our programme and the commitment required before they sign up.'

It continued, 'All players and parents are invited twice a year to discuss the progress of their son at a parents evening, and written reports are given to feed back the coaches' thoughts, observations and recommendations.'

Coventry's demands are no different to those of most academies. They are merely trying to find a way to meet the target of the 10,000 hours of training time it supposedly takes to develop an elite sportsman. The academy match programme wasn't their design and it is currently being amended to allow academies to play matches against local centre of excellence teams in order to cut down on excessive travel times.

The pressure of playing in a centre of excellence can be just as demanding. Nathan Wall, who also lives in the West Midlands, signed up to play for local Football League club Walsall at the age of nine. He was with the club for five years. His dad Steven went into it with his eyes wide open, 'I had started a junior club with another coach which we called FC Premier when Nathan had started playing football at six years old. I wanted to learn how to coach, so I took a couple of coaching badges and you think you start to learn a bit about the game, but I had no idea about youth development really.'

Like the other parents, he thought Nathan was on his way to stardom. 'I thought once he's in, he's going to end up playing professional football. All the other parents were the same. There is a fear factor with parents, too. If the club says jump, you ask how high. If your boy misses a training session, you worry if that will go against him. Nathan played with injuries and didn't want to let on.'

For the first three years Nathan loved it. The coach was very encouraging and Nathan developed a tight-knit group of friends. His team were kept together from under 9 to 11. In the early days it was all about technique. 'He gained a lot of experience and technically he became an excellent player,' said Steven.

But then things started to change. Once they switched to 11-a-side soccer at 12 years old the matches became more serious and Nathan felt under pressure. He stopped enjoying his football – and felt the weight of having boys coming into the squad and replacing his team-mates one by one. 'Sometimes there were 20 of them playing with the 12 already selected – there were too many players,' said Nathan. 'The team spirit had gone.'

Nathan completely lost his appetite for the game, 'I just felt pressure all the time, there was no vote of confidence from the coaches and most of the time it was just criticism. If I made a mistake during a game I felt that the club were going to think, "Well, we don't want him at the club no more", so every game you're playing for the shirt. I wasn't myself anymore. I started to be moody, and I just didn't have any more desire. Every weekend, I just didn't want to get up and play. That's how I was really feeling at the time.'

Nonetheless, like the Craigs, the Walls kept on going. Nathan even played a game at Bristol Rovers when he was ill. 'I wasn't feeling that well, but I travelled there and only got 10 minutes of football.' How did that feel? 'Bitter,' said Nathan. 'You feel you're not wanted anymore. After that, I thought, "I don't know why I'm at this club because I'm not enjoying the football and I'd rather be at another club".'

After another six hours of travelling time just to play 10 minutes of football Steven felt he had to say something. 'I told the coach I thought it was wrong to take up so much of the boy's days for so little football,' said Steven. 'But I could see which way it was going.' Where Nathan was heading was out of the door.

In common with many clubs, Walsall refused to comment on Nathan's experience or discuss details of any of their individual youth players.

'Desire' is a big word in football. There's the desire to win, to keep running, pushing, powering on through the wind and rain. Digging out results. Driving on. It doesn't necessarily mean the desire to develop and show off silky skills: step overs, drag backs, 'Cruyff' turns to make monkeys out of defenders, open up goal-scoring opportunities to thrill and inspire the fans. No, traditional desire is an attitude born of the old days when strong, powerful players were needed to plough through the muddy bogs that passed for pitches, even those at professional clubs. That sort of desire made sense – was needed. Still is, apparently.

Jamie (not his real name) played at a local Football League club centre of excellence for six years. His early experiences mirrored those of Ryan Craig and Nathan Wall. His dad, Simon (again, not his real name) described his coach as 'inspirational'. He was proud to see his son sporting the club colours. 'He was taught the basic skills and it was fun and the kids seemed to enjoy it.' Although, again, they found the travelling a chore, it was bearable because the small-sided games ensured they got lots of action and Jamie seemed really happy. Simon also liked the discipline – players were taught to respect the referee and to be polite. His coach even stopped a match one day to berate parents for their behaviour after questioning a referee's decision. It was all about respect.

But again at 12, things changed. 'The training became more and more focussed on strength and endurance, observed Simon, 'Individual brilliance was almost frowned upon as dangerous to the team. The work ethic was king.' In training, if players stopped moving or running they were ordered to do five press-ups on the spot. Children aged 12 and 13 were made to do endurance training until they either vomited or gave up. 'It was made clear to them that the club did not want players who gave up. So they ran until they were sick for fear of being released,' said Simon.

Commerciality also kicked in. Parents were ordered to pay £150 a year for club kit and to pay extras to fund overseas trips. 'It was so the club could make money or at least recoup the money they were spending on youth development.' Feedback was also less forthcoming. 'We weren't encouraged to ask how the players – our

children – were getting on,' said Simon. 'If you criticised or questioned anything it was made clear you and your son would be asked
to leave the academy.'

Resentment built up among parents – and eventually the players.
Jamie began to get injured more and more frequently. The injuries
meant he didn't have to train or play in matches. 'I see now that he
was magnifying the usual aches and pains that athletes get because the
football just wasn't fun any more,' said Simon, who wondered why his
son would go down injured and not even try to carry on. He seemed
happy to be substituted and just watch the match. 'Fortunately he was
a sensible lad who kept going at his schoolwork, otherwise I dread to
think what would have happened,' added Simon. 'Well, I do know
actually. We would have pulled out of the centre of excellence.'

I asked sports scientist Rick Fenoglio if there was any merit in
running boys until they are sick. He responded, 'Only if you want to
put them off sport forever. I have heard coaches say they do it for
psychological reasons – but there is no evidence to say you will make
them tougher on a football pitch. It may work in the military, but not
in sport.'

Fenoglio explained the 'four corners' approach to coaching: the
physical, psychological, tactical and technical aspects that apply to
football. 'Smart coaches will integrate the psychological and physical
criteria – the toughening up – in technical sessions, so it is combined.
The real problem in academies is they don't have enough time; the
integration of all these aspects should be key.'

In terms of welfare, the parent of a current Premier League player
told me that clubs like 'low maintenance' players. In other words, players who won't cause them any problems – whether that be with their
family background, or problems in their personal life or at school.

The better clubs work hard at keeping any problems at bay. Aston
Villa, for example, make sure any education problems are nipped in
the bud as soon as possible. 'We build relationships with schools and
if there is a problem with a boy, if he is becoming troublesome or has
switched off because he thinks he is going to become a footballer,
we contact his school within seven days,' said Brian Jones. 'We will
support the school in whatever way we feel is right. Occasionally, we

have withdrawn players from matches with parental backing. It sounds tough, but it works.'

The club's education and welfare officer, Paul Brackwell, is a former Buckinghamshire schoolteacher and has managed the England Schoolboys team. He believes that 11 years after the introduction of the *Charter for Quality* the academy system has bedded in. He feels that the education provision for 16 to 18 year olds has improved dramatically. 'Psychologically they all think they are going to be professional footballers. So we work hard in the nine to 16 age group to ensure the football side of things is kept to a low profile. We don't make any promises and ask parents and schools not to make a big deal of the fact a boy is coming here to train with us. Between the ages of 14 and 16 it is particularly important we work with the school to make sure the player concentrates on getting the best GCSEs he can. It is important they have something to fall back on and that a possible career in football doesn't go to their heads. I am here to prepare them if they fail so they have a second career route.'

But Brian Jones is unhappy that the academy match programme means boys and their parents are spending so long travelling to play games instead of working on their skills. 'Is it right that a nine-year-old has to travel from Birmingham to Middlesbrough and back on a Sunday just to play 30 minutes of football?' he asks. 'I think it is absolutely ludicrous – but that's what's happening. As a club we have considered not participating in the match programme because of this.'

Not all clubs are as proactive as Aston Villa. Dave Woollaston, teacher and some time ESFA coach, says relationships between schools and clubs vary enormously. 'At best it is very good, at worst it is terrible,' he said. It is a point many parents may wish to consider before sending their children to play in a football club academy or centre of excellence. 'Parents believe they have to do what the academy or centre of excellence tells them,' said Woollaston. 'I don't think parents know how much power they have. They have choices but are often frightened that the club will let their lads go if they go against the club's wishes.'

Woollaston is particularly concerned about the clubs that try to dissuade their academy players from participating in school sports. 'Some academies frown upon anything that they consider risky.

They often tell boys that they cannot play for their school teams. The boys are being told what they can and cannot do.

'The boys will get kudos among their peer group, who will look up to them because they have signed with a professional football club. But when they can't play, not just football, but other sports like cricket, rugby, basketball, canoeing, let alone activities like rock climbing, skiing and ice skating, they miss out. It makes me feel sad. I like to produce rounded pupils with a good attitude to sport. Preventing children from participating in the social life of the school, to me, seems wrong.'

This is an attitude the football industry denies holding. Graham Hawkins, the Football League's head of player development, claims that clubs are merely concerned that boys don't play too much football. He says, 'they are allowed to play for their schools but what we ask is that they don't do it secretly. It is not good for a lad to play a school game and then turn up an hour later to train. Some of the clubs are now giving the boys diaries – so they can keep a note of what they have been doing because we don't want them over-training. The clubs should inform the schools about the diaries so they can be shown to the teachers. The schools have got to monitor what they are doing.'

The Football League's deputy operations manager Michael Tattersall insists there is no pressure to stop playing football at school. 'We don't dictate these matters. It is permitted. But they have to work out their own local solution to it.' He claims not to understand why many parents think that their boys cannot play for the school team.

At Middlesbrough Dave Parnaby believes there is nothing wrong with asking players and parents to understand the sacrifices their boys need to make to play at elite football academies – and the commitment expected of them. 'If a boy comes to us he is making a commitment to train five hours a week and play a game on Sunday. It is an excellence programme. We say, "If you are prepared to sacrifice your time and effort to achieve that, then sign this form. If you don't want to do that – if you want to play for the school – then maybe it's best that you don't sign."

'We don't mind them playing for the school as long as we know. Sometimes their teachers encourage them to play and say, "no one will know". Then they come to us and don't tell us. So what I say to the parents is, "If you choose to play for the school, tell us and we'll not expect you to come to training – and if you play for the school on Friday, then you'll not play on Sunday". It is a choice. It is a voluntary registration. Some can handle it, others haven't got that level of dedication.'

However, Dave Woollaston spins this argument around on its head. He suggests that sometimes attending a football academy actually makes boys too tired to do their schoolwork. 'I see boys who are physically very tired. We had one boy who was travelling a good hour-and-a-half to an academy. On matchdays he would have to travel a further two hours to reach the ground where he was playing. His travel time alone on that day was seven hours. I don't know how much football he played that day – 60 minutes maximum – but he spent seven hours getting there and back. It's madness.'

Woollaston advises boys against withdrawing from school sport, but acknowledges his influence is minimal. 'They aren't going to listen to me. I'm just a teacher of 36 years standing with a fair bit of experience in youth and schools football. What do I know? They listen to the club instead.'

The bigger concern for Woollaston is that he sees boys relegate their education to the subs bench; 'They don't really put the time and effort into their school work and so underachieve academically, and when the club turns and says, as it does to the vast majority of boys, I'm sorry but you aren't good enough, they haven't got the qualifications to fall back on.'

One club that has developed its own progressive policy of making their young recruits feel at home is Manchester United. You'll also struggle to find better facilities than at Manchester United's training ground at Carrington in the Cheshire countryside. There I meet Tony Whelan, the club's assistant academy director, who shows me around. It isn't just the fantastic facilities at Carrington – it's the ethos. The young players are taught to look you in the eye and offer a firm handshake. The players welcome me to their academy with unerring politeness. It is almost disturbing, yet they don't know who I am or that I am a journalist. They're not turning on the PR charm to impress – it is just how they are.

Pictures of past United legends adorn the corridor walls: Duncan Edwards, Bobby Charlton, Denis Law, George Best, Bryan Robson, Eric Cantona, David Beckham, Ryan Giggs – it is a mighty long list ... and finally a silhouette marked, 'You?'

It is a relaxed atmosphere – deliberately so. 'The academic word for it is "holistic",' says Whelan. 'The emotional side is as important as the physical. They can have fun with their team-mates and engage with the coaches and staff who are there to help them to get better.'

The club has railed against the mandatory eight-a-side games played in academies by 9 to 11 year olds, and instead, with the help of sports scientist Rick Fenoglio at Manchester Metropolitan University, has developed a four-a-side game as part of its approach to nurturing new talent.

'We try to create an environment that is non-threatening and player-centred,' said Whelan. 'They need to know that it is OK to make mistakes. We are removing the fear factor here. It should be an exciting time. When they play on a Sunday it should be the happiest time of their lives. They only get one go at being young boys. We want them to make the most of it.'

Finding your way to these academies can be difficult. Manchester United's training ground is down a narrow lane, for example you'd never find it if you didn't know where to look. Manchester City's new academy centre is nearby. Villa's is 16 miles from inner city Aston, a poor suburb of Birmingham, and Middlesbrough's Rockcliffe Park is located in Hurworth, some 15 miles from their home at the Riverside. England's top clubs have escaped to the country – but how accessible are they to parents? Not everyone has a car or can bunk off work early to whisk their kids to the training ground in time. It raises an uncomfortable question for this traditionally working-class sport.

'You used to recruit most players from inner cities,' said Brian Jones, who is keen to heap praise on the parents who schlep back and forth to training and matches. 'The commitment from players and parents is superb.' Then he makes a shocking observation. 'Today, ours is a very middle-class academy. We have players coming from places like Gloucester, which is a 180-mile round trip.'

While that seems a long way to travel it is within the permitted travel time rules. But some clubs are prepared to disregard the distance rule, a sensible welfare measure designed to protect children from excessive tiredness during the school week. As we have already learned the *Charter for Quality* insists that boys under 12 years old are not allowed to travel for more than an hour to an academy or centre of excellence, and boys aged between 12 to 16 years old shouldn't spend more than 90 minutes travelling each way. Each player's registration is checked by Premier League or Football League inspectors (usually via an online system such as Routeplanner or similar), to ensure that the distance between the boy's home and the academy doesn't exceed the estimated travel time.

While this can be a moot point – getting a few miles across London, for instance, can be different to a long trek down a quiet motorway in the suburbs – the rules are there to be adhered to. However, some clubs collude with parents to circumvent this child protection measure.

I have heard of a 13-year-old boy travelling from Leicester to London on his own via public transport to attend a prominent Premier League academy. A 14 year old was travelling from Worcester to an academy in the north-west of England – and you cannot make that sort of journey along the M5 and M6 in 90 minutes. In both these cases the address of a local relative was used to evade detection.

However, what follows is a shocking case of football club collusion, parental irresponsibility and weak enforcement of the regulations resulting in real problems for the boy in question. At nine years of age, Sam (not his real name) started attending a prominent Premier League club academy that was 88 miles from his home, an estimated 1 hour and 45 minutes travelling time. Bearing in mind the boy would travel during the early evening rush hour, it is safe to assume this was the bare minimum amount of time it could take.

His father, a former professional footballer, had taken Sam to several local academies and hadn't liked what he had seen. 'Sixty kids turned up at one and were playing a massive 30-a-side on an Astroturf pitch so I thought, "Not coming back here again". At another, we turned up at 6 p.m., the coach wasn't there, hadn't got his bibs and cones out, by the time he got things sorted they only had half an hour's training, so that was no good, and at another club the coaching was good but the facilities were very poor.'

Instead he decided to take Sam to an academy that was outside his permitted area. He was impressed, 'the facilities and the coaching stood out. The club had a good reputation in youth development. We knew it was a long way to travel three times a week, but I was prepared to give my kid the best go – and the best shot at the time, in my opinion, was that particular club.'

The club knew it was against the rules for Sam to travel that far – so they found a way around the rules. On matchdays, he competed under another name with a local address. The inspectors never picked this up – how would they? Sam was allowed to play.

I asked Sam's dad whether he knew if the academy was outside the permitted travel regulations: 'To be honest with you, yes, but I thought we could get away with it. Looking back with hindsight I would probably say it was a mistake.'

It was a tiring schedule for Sam, 'I'd eat and do some homework in the car on the way. I'd train, get home at about 10.30 p.m. and complete any homework I hadn't done, and this was when I was 12. I was really tired. I struggled to get up some mornings, and once or twice I'd ask for the day off from school.'

Amazingly, this carried on for three years until a coach mistakenly (from the club's point of view) put Sam's real name on a form. It was detected by the Premier League's inspectors, and Sam was prevented from attending the academy. The club was duly fined. When asked about the incident both the Premier League and the club refused to comment, insisting it was a private matter.

However, a letter addressed to Sam by the club's academy director in September 2000, to thank him for his efforts read, 'Sadly, we have to conform to the rules,' and goes on to praise his '...wonderful parental support ... which will ensure you get the help you need.' There is no apology for conspiring to break the rules with the help of his dad, who encouraged him to lie in order to work his way around a child protection measure designed for his own welfare.

Subsequently, Sam joined another academy where, again, he gave his total commitment. However, that club released him at 16.

Looking back he said, 'I had been at academy level since I was ten, and I have nothing to show for it. In retrospect I wish I had done a few things differently. I didn't concentrate on school much. I just thought I had to turn up at school but that football was always going to be my outcome.'

Mike Foster at the FA Premier League acknowledges that it is difficult for inspectors to check if clubs choose to use false names and/or addresses. However, he reiterated that all player registrations are thoroughly examined. 'They are closely monitored. Every registration is religiously checked to make sure the estimated journey time between the player's home and the academy is within the rules, and if it is outside the requirements it will be rejected,' says Foster. 'In the last seven years we have dealt with 62 cases where parents have appealed against the decision we have taken. The majority of cases will be accepted. This may be because they can go to a development centre or the academy is reachable within the limits – but we will also tie-in strict conditions, like having the headmaster's approval.'

However, it is known that some clubs want to see the time and travel rule scrapped. They believe it prevents them from signing the players they want – regardless of where they live – and many would welcome the chance to open local development centres anywhere around the country so that they can train players near where they live and move them to their main academy at 16 years old.

'It is still a minority of our clubs that want to abolish the distance rule,' insists Foster. 'The *Charter for Quality* was based around the best interests of the child and that is a principle we want to be true to going forward.'

But the top clubs, in particular, have good reasons as to why they want the rule scrapped. At present, despite clubs being able to forge official links with foreign clubs and even set up their own academies abroad, they cannot set up academies elsewhere in England. Doing so would give them a better chance of getting the best boys from all over the country into their academies without having to pay fees to acquire them from other academies and centres of excellence. This is a practice know as 'predatory' activity.

CHAPTER 6

PREDATORS AND POACHERS

The smiling face said it all. The Monday morning after the Saturday when John Bostock, aged 15 years and 287 days, made his first-team debut for Crystal Palace on 27 October 2007 – the team he supported and had a season ticket to watch – was back at school in Blackfriars ... so too, were the press.

Cue the photos of blazer-wearing Bostock at the blackboard with the word 'debut' chalked up on it. Outside, he posed to play head tennis in the playground.

Every boy's dream? Of course. Bostock had only played 18 minutes of first-team football – but few 15 year olds get to do that. Special? For sure. Former Palace manager Peter Taylor, sacked just days earlier, said, 'Bostock will not just be a good player, he will be a great player.'

At school, the dampeners doused any fears of premature stardom going to Bostock's head. 'We're very proud of him,' bubbled Neil McGregor, deputy head teacher and head of PE at the London Nautical School in Blackfriars. 'He has a lot of humility, he's very honest and there is no danger of him ever becoming a Big Time Charlie. His feet are firmly on the ground.'

Academically bright – university potential apparently – and a gifted all-round athlete, he even held the Lambeth Schools' 110 metres hurdles record.

Crystal Palace manager, Neil Warnock, was equally fulsome in praise of Bostock's stepfather, Mick Brown. 'Mick is incredibly level-headed and he has been wonderful to deal with. John is a smashing lad and we want to build a team around him.'

Fast-forward to July 2008 – and the comments coming from the south London club are not quite so glowing. The reason? Bostock had decided to sign a five-year deal with north London Premier League side Tottenham Hotspur, who were entitled to sign Bostock as his registration period with Palace had ended and he was able to sign for whichever club he wanted.

However, as the club who had developed him, Crystal Palace, a Championship level club, were entitled to claim compensation for the time they had spent coaching this prodigious talent. But the clubs couldn't agree on a fee – so the matter was referred to a tribunal.

At the hearing, Palace proposed they should receive £2 million plus a further £2.5 million when Bostock, by then England's Under-17s captain, had played 40 matches for Tottenham. They based their estimate on the £5 million deal that had taken 17-year-old Aaron Ramsey from Cardiff City to Arsenal a few weeks earlier.

But the committee settled on an initial compensation fee of £700,000 to be paid by Tottenham to Palace, with increments of £250,000 after Bostock has made 5, 10, 20, 30 and 40 first-team appearances – up to a total of £1.25 million – plus a further £200,000 if Bostock makes his England senior first-team debut and a 15 per cent share of any profit made by Tottenham if they sell him on.

This was substantially less than Palace had wanted. Crystal Palace chairman Simon Jordan was outraged. 'I feel mugged and brutalised,' he fumed. 'It is scandalous. This sends a message to smaller clubs. Why bother to bring players through if the compensation does not reflect the work that has gone in? This sends out a bad precedent.'

For all its fine words, one thing the *Charter for Quality* didn't include was a solution to one of the age-old pressing concerns of youth development – clubs nabbing each other's players. Sometimes this is done perfectly legally, as Tottenham showed in the Bostock case. Sometimes it is achieved using more devious, and notoriously difficult-to-prove methods such as approaching the player and parents directly, 'unsettling them' as it is sometimes called, then offering nothing in compensation. There is a word for it in football – it's called poaching.

The charter's optimistic call for 'quality and unity' failed to deal with this underhand practice, which breeds resentment and contempt in equal measure among the clubs being raided by so-called 'predator' clubs. In fact, given that it granted new powers to clubs to sign more boys at a much younger age than ever before, it actually prompted an increase in just this kind of activity.

In fairness, the charter clearly establishes the ground rules by saying, 'A club may not approach, directly or indirectly, any player registered with another centre of excellence or football academy.' But the desire for success in English football today means that clubs are not content with grubbing around in an attempt to snare the youngest boys possible, but have also been avaricious in gobbling up each other's best players. Whatever the reasons, the fact is England's professional football clubs trade boys for millions of pounds. It is youth development's most entangled moral maze. Different people have differing views – you pay your money and you take your choice.

'You'll always have nickers and pinchers,' said Dave Richardson, the former head of youth development at the Premier League, who had hoped what he calls 'the duckers and divers' would have disappeared when the academy system came into being and that it would offer a fresh start.

'Everybody's done things they regret and I would be the first to admit that in my career I am not proud of some of the things I did as a coach and a developer,' he admitted. 'We created a situation where we said, "look, the slates are clean, let's start again". Unfortunately, football is a selfish industry, you have to have a certain amount of selfishness in your nature, because you've got to look after number one.'

But to Richardson's disappointment, the 'duckers and divers' have not left English football. If anything, there are more of them. Richardson also said he had never had to deal with a youth player's agent during his time in club youth development (between 1965 and 1994) before he joined the Premier League. Nowadays, it is common for talented junior and youth players to have agents bargaining on their behalf.

It is small wonder that this thoroughly decent man, with an impeccable reputation in the game, opted for an administrative job prior to retiring in 2006 – although many people will be pleased to see this popular figure within English football back as chairman of the Professional Football Coaches Association.

Logic told him and others that, with 10,000 boys signed up to academies or centres of excellence, the movement between clubs could only increase – even if some of the charter's rules were designed to negate poaching.

Players now have a 'window of opportunity', a period of time between registrations, where they can go on trial at another club or just simply check out other clubs' facilities before deciding whether to stay put or move on. This offers them genuine freedom of choice. Other rules, such as the time and travel rule, limit the geographical range from which clubs can pick up rival club's players.

However, in terms of straightforward clear governance on the movement of youngsters from club to club there are few rules. Instead, it has been left to the Football League – and therefore the clubs themselves – to establish a compensation payment system to set fees when the clubs can't come to their own agreement. Initially, this tribunal panel was called the Football League Appeals Committee (FLAC), but it is now known as the Professional Football Compensation Committee (PCCC), which comprises an independent chairman, appointees from the Premier League and the Football League (as applicable), an appointee of the Professional Footballers' Association (PFA) and another from the League Managers' Association (LMA).

The panel listens to the cases put by both clubs: the club losing the player, which provides an estimate of how much it has cost to develop him and their opinion of his future potential, and the buying club, who will lay out their case.

Anecdotally, one interviewee summed it up like this, 'the selling club will say he is a world beater, the buying club will insist he's average.' Discuss.

The panel will then set a compensation fee, which often, as in the Bostock case, includes increments to be paid by the club gaining the player if he achieves certain targets, such as making his senior first-team debut, and reaching a certain number of first-team appearances, making his international debut and maybe even a sell-on clause.

In all but name this is a transfer fee. A small levy goes to the PFA's Players Benevolent Fund, but none of the money goes to the player or seeps back to grass roots football – for example to the junior club or school that might have given the player his first taste of football. The money stays firmly within professional football – and there is no requirement for it to go anywhere else.

While the payments may suit football's own eco-system, constantly losing your best players can have a demoralising effect on academy staff. Many coaches have left the game dispirited, even questioning in which direction football's moral compass is pointing.

One such coach is Andy Beaglehole, who was academy director at Oldham Athletic and had previously been a youth coach at Leeds United and Middlesbrough, before leaving the professional game in 2002.

He was disillusioned and depressed over developing players, only to lose them on a regular basis to bigger, richer rival clubs, who could afford to pay the compensation fees being set by the FLAC. Indeed, one of his last duties at Oldham was to put together a compensation claim for losing future England defender Micah Richards, who was 13 at the time, and had left them to join Manchester City.

Interviewed in 2002, Beaglehole wanted to say his piece and get out of professional football – preferring now to work in a college football programme, free of the 'nicking and pinching'.

He explained the modus operandi of the clubs who routinely raid smaller club academies for their better players, the so-called 'predator' clubs. 'We've had an outstanding youngster in our Under-9s this year [at Oldham] and, when we've played other clubs in the north-west we've had instances of him being approached by a scout from another club,' explained Beaglehole. 'In one case the scout was asked to leave. We reported it, and took it further with letters and tried to collect evidence. But the boy left us at the end of the year and now we're fighting to get some compensation for him. It is frustrating, not just for me but for all the staff involved,' said Beaglehole. He also dismissed the idea that this activity is confined to academy staff level, 'Our compensation claims go to the secretary of the club we're pursuing, so obviously it is discussed at boardroom level.'

A glance at the list of FLAC compensation rulings for June 2002 – which were shown to me by an official of the Football League, but are no longer available to the public – support Beaglehole's assessment of the situation. Players as young as nine years old were effectively being transferred from one club to another for fees sometimes up to tens of thousands of pounds. For older boys – in the 14- to 16-year-old age range – whose future is more certain, compensation is likely to rise to hundreds of thousands and even millions of pounds.

One name that stands out from the FLAC list is Liam Ridgewell, a future England Under-21 international, who moved from West Ham to Aston Villa in 2001 at the age of 16. Villa paid £50,000, plus four subsequent payments of £100,000 each for 10, 20, 30, and 40 appearances he made for the club, plus 15 per cent of any future sale. Altogether, Ridgewell made 79 appearances for Villa before being sold to Birmingham City in 2007 for £2 million. In total, Villa paid £750,000 for the player, but made an eventual £1.25 million profit when they sold him. Nice one.

However, most of the players on the list appear to have faded from professional football including a 15 year old who moved from Swansea to Southampton for £500,000.

Youth football is governed by some shocking statistics – 75 per cent of the players who sign a contract for a full-time scholarship at 16 leave the game before they are 21. Only one in six who sign contracts at the age of 18 are in the game for longer than three years. Given these statistics, clubs want to avoid paying big transfer fees for players who are not guaranteed to succeed. So they look to recruit younger players who will, of course, carry lower compensation fees. The FLAC list includes an under-11 player who moved to Manchester United from Preston North End for fees which could total £136,000, and an under-10 player who joined Birmingham City from West Bromwich Albion for £35,000.

Of course, paying a fee for a youngster is something of a gambler's punt. 'A friend of mine who is an academy director mentioned to me that as part of his budget he'd set aside £10,000 for compensation because they'd be looking at lads aged nine or 10 from some of the smaller clubs round his region,' said Beaglehole. 'On the present rate [in 2002] of £2,500 for a 9 year old, he could get four under-9s or two under-12s, maybe at £5,000 each. We would much rather have the player at Oldham Athletic than £5,000.'

Although there is nothing illegal in clubs paying the compensation fees, predatory activity has a morale sapping effect on youth development staff. A former academy director, who didn't want to be named (unlike Beaglehole, he is still in the game), told me it was 'heartbreaking … frustrating … and soul destroying,' to lose players. He is in no doubt that some clubs, as he put it, 'are affluent enough and have a philosophy whereby they believe that they simply *have* to recruit the best talent in the game. The system favours the rich,' he added, 'who will get stronger and the less affluent will suffer unless the compensation levels are used as a deterrent to prevent cherry picking.'

It is a situation the Football League is mindful of – after all, it is mainly their member clubs who are vulnerable prey to the big spending predators. 'There are some predatory clubs out there who can undermine the good work that follows on at other clubs who want to develop players,' noted Jim Briden, the Football League's youth development business manager. 'The youth staff within a club don't necessarily get their investment back – sometimes the money stays elsewhere within the club.'

Glyn Harding, who worked at Shrewsbury Town's centre of excellence where they developed the likes of Manchester City and England goalkeeper Joe Hart and Newcastle United midfielder Danny Guthrie among others, and later at Wolverhampton Wanderers' academy as education and welfare officer, also became disillusioned. 'We never got a penny for any of the lads we developed at Shrewsbury,' said Harding, who now works as a senior lecturer in sports coaching science at the University of Worcester. 'You start thinking, "what is this centre of excellence structure all about?" Is it about small clubs putting kids in the shop window for bigger clubs to come and cherry pick?'

'Clubs are now better at getting boys under contract – but it was soul destroying back then. At Shrewsbury, we could have developed a youth system like they have at Crewe Alexandra, where they develop good players and sell some on to reinvest in future youth development.'

Harding reckons that the players who find themselves sucked up by the predator clubs can also lose out. 'At least Joe Hart got into Shrewsbury's first team and got some games under his belt. The problem for many boys is they move on to bigger clubs and don't get first-team opportunities, so they don't progress.'

Although it is never admitted, there is a feeling that fees have sometimes been set high in order to deter predator clubs. 'Nard amused' joked the *Sun* headline, after Manchester United were ordered to pay initial fees of £200,000 that could have risen to £1.5 million each for two Wolves 14 year olds, Daniel Nardiello and Kris Taylor, at a FLAC tribunal held in July 2000. It was suggested that Sir Alex Ferguson was far from impressed with the outcome.

Wolves had justified their high valuations by saying that both players were quite advanced for their age, for example more so than Robbie Keane, a player they had sold to Coventry City for £6 million in 1999. Like a number of other clubs, Wolves subsequently banned scouts representing some clubs, including Manchester United, from attending their academy matches.

Although neither Nardiello nor Taylor made it at Manchester United, many of England's top players moved – sometimes controversially – in similar circumstances. Arsenal were ordered to pay £2 million for signing Jermaine Pennant from Notts County; West Ham forked out £1.69 million when they took Jermain Defoe from Charlton Athletic – ultimately selling him on for £7 million.

Despite its shortcomings, many believe that without the compensation system there would be more accusations of poaching – a charge that is dealt with by the Football Association. One of the first FLAC cases to set a compensation fee involved Manchester United, who were fined £50,000 for signing David Brown, a Bolton schoolboy international centre forward, while he was under contract at Oldham Athletic in 1996. United were ordered to pay Oldham £75,000 compensation by the Football Association. At an FA hearing a month earlier, United were found guilty of making an illegal approach for Matthew Wicks, a talented England youth defender who had attended the FA National School at Lilleshall and had joined them from Arsenal. They escaped having to pay a fine, as Wicks opted to return to his former club.

Mike Foster, general secretary of the Premier League, is clear in his opinion of the rules on poaching, 'If clubs breach rules they are brought to account and if found guilty they face a range of penalties. But we need a complainant before we can take action. We have clubs contact us each year without exception complaining that another club has made an improper approach to one of their players. We will investigate that complaint and write to the club. The complainant will then have the option of accepting the apology, explanation or stance taken by the other club or ask for them to be charged. If we decide there is sufficient evidence, we will charge the club. But very few clubs will go that far.'

Some do though – including Leeds United chairman Ken Bates, who accused his former club, Chelsea, of making an illegal approach – or 'tapping up' as its known – to three Leeds trainees. 'Leeds challenged Chelsea in relation to what they were doing – and the clubs agreed a settlement for a significant sum of money,' said Foster. 'Leeds were happy with the money they were offered. We were not content with that and demanded assurances from Chelsea that all staff involved in recruitment were subject to an appropriate training programme.'

Two of the players, Michael Woods and Tom Taiwo, moved to Chelsea, but the third teenager, Danny Rose, opted to stay with Leeds.

Smaller clubs feel they stand little chance of keeping their star assets – who, when they move on to a top club with deep pockets, are not always being offered opportunities, but are brought in and loaned out. Scott Sinclair was a product of the Bristol Rovers youth system, having joined them aged nine and, like John Bostock at Crystal Palace, made his senior first-team debut at the age of 15. Chelsea signed Sinclair in July 2005, and in November 2005 a tribunal awarded Rovers compensation of £200,000 with a possible extra £750,000 to come, depending on his level of success at his new club. Chelsea will also have to pay Bristol Rovers 15 per cent if they sell him. On the face of it this could be a lucrative deal for the Rovers, but at the time of writing (April 2009), Sinclair has made just four first-team appearances for Chelsea and has been loaned out to five different clubs, so Rovers are left waiting for their windfall … if it ever comes.

'I don't have a problem with the concept of compensation,' said Mike Foster. 'It is fair that if a club has spent time developing a boy and he decides to join another club then his first club is entitled to compensation. How compensation is assessed is another matter. I can understand there might be different points of view.'

Continuing with his relentless call for an increase in quality of young players, Sir Trevor Brooking believes the trading has became more desperate because the very talented players are becoming harder to find. He believes that if the young boys were coached in FA centres, and moved to clubs later, trading at the younger end of the scale, at least, would diminish. 'The players are commodities to them [the clubs],' said Brooking. 'We had discussions and said, "Why don't you let us [the FA] develop these boys up to 11 years old and then let the clubs come in later? We could fund the coaches who could be affiliated to the club, but not identified as their coaches. They could work with our FA Charter Standard clubs locally and develop them that way."'

Brooking added, 'Football League clubs don't want to be raided – so you can see why they want to sell players for as much money as possible – but the top clubs don't want to pay over the top. They go looking abroad now because they don't want to take the chance and spend money on players who might not make it. I can see both sides of things. But if we don't do something about developing our players I think we will be in a really bad position. I don't think the money will be there and I don't think our boys will be good enough.'

Aside from the sanctions there are fears that the fees crank up the pressure for the boys, which can distract them from their educational and social development. The idea of boys being traded doesn't sit well with many people, including the parents who often don't realise their children will be bought and sold in this way. Andrea, for example, the mother of six-year-old Jack, who was 'culled' by a Premier League club, was 'horrified' to discover that if they had signed him at nine years old Jack could have been sold to another club.

Dave Woollaston, of the English Schools FA, likens this trade to 'child trafficking'. 'There's no payment to the players, it's only payment to the clubs,' he said. 'It's a trafficking fee, if you like. They're using their young children as a commodity. Pretty horrible thing to think about, isn't it?'

The word 'trafficking' usually carries a sinister implication of illegality. 'Yes, I hold by that,' insisted Woollaston. 'Ask yourself who gets the most out of it? If I thought the academy system was giving more to all these young players than it was taking out, I would change my views … but it's not … it is there for one sole purpose … and that is to find top-level footballers, and if that means paying for them, so be it.'

Somewhat surprisingly, Brian Jones, Aston Villa's academy director, agrees with Woollaston's comments that the fees amount to 'child trafficking'. 'That's absolutely spot on,' said Jones. 'The game has devised a system where we look to recruit boys as young as eight into academy football, which I am against. I wouldn't personally like to see a boy at the club until the age of 12, when they have moved into senior school. At that point, as a recruiter, you have a better idea of that boy's talent.

'Most parents don't know that if their son wants to sign for Aston Villa from another club then we have to pay a fee to the smaller club who will recover compensation for the time they have spent training him. The tribunal fees are getting higher and there will come a stage where clubs will not sign a youngster because he costs too much.'

However, that view doesn't get much sympathy among Football League clubs. 'The problem is that if players could leave when they wanted there would be no incentive to develop them,' reasoned Michael Tattersall, deputy operations director at the Football League. 'The ideal outcome is that clubs develop local players and get them through to their own first team. I have yet to hear of a club that is happy to see one of their talented players move on before they turn professional.'

Despite the large amounts of money that seem to be available to buy young players, none of it gets back to the grass roots. 'If a Premier League club makes a payment to a Football League club, where does that money go? Bigger wages?' asks Dave Woollaston. 'It's not ring-fenced for the youngsters. It may even be spent on recruiting players, which makes it harder for other boys at the academy to get a chance of first-team football.

'The money just doesn't get down to where the boys come from,' he complains. 'Very few clubs or schools have professional fundraisers. It'll be the guy whose job it is to coach the team who makes all the phone calls, who is dealing with the administration, who suddenly finds his team is successful and he needs a few more quid. He either puts his hand in his own pocket or he goes searching for sponsorship. The money in the academies doesn't ever come back to grass roots. It is spent and it disappears.'

Therefore, the situation seems to be that because professional clubs can't make the books balance, there is no money left to plough back into grass roots football, the place where many footballers first learn their trade. Professional clubs don't see a problem with this. 'Clubs outside the Football League don't have to contribute to player development in the same way as league clubs because they don't offer a career path to being a full-time professional player,' said Michael Tattersall. 'Development is a costly business. There are no profits; it all gets burnt up in players' wages.'

But surely the system would have more credibility if some of the compensation money was fed back to the permanently parched grass roots game – maybe in the form of a levy? 'I think grass roots clubs actually understand their role and the professional clubs' role in the game, and coaches at this level regard success as the ability to develop a player that is actually good enough to join a professional football club,' added Tattersall.

These arguments do not sit well with non-League football. Aside from the junior clubs, who frequently find themselves raided for their better players with nothing going back to them in the opposite direction, semi-professional or even professional clubs in the national Conference League and its feeder divisions are completely cut out of the compensation system. 'Last year I put an estimated 850 hours of free time into administrating this league,' said Andy Barnett, chairman of the Midland Junior Premier Football League (MJPFL), a youth development league for, as the name implies, Midlands-based, non-League clubs. The MJPFL, which began in 2004, has divisions at all age levels from under-12 through to under-18 and, for the 2008-09 season, had 108 teams from 47 different clubs participating – some 2,500 players in total.

'Aside from the many players who are now playing semi-professional football we have had 12 players who have been offered contracts at professional clubs and produced four England Under-16 internationals and one Scottish Under-16 international,' said Barnett. 'Roughly one-third of our players have been at professional academies or centres of excellence. We provide a safety net for these players who are released and often don't have a club to go to and don't want to drop straight into local junior football because the gap is so wide. Our league is ideal for them.'

A smile spreads around Barnett's face at the suggestion that the professional game says there are no costs attached to running non-League youth development programmes. 'Tell that to the clubs who play in this league – to coaches who pay their own fees to take coaching badges, for the child protection courses we insist they must take, to the cost of running transport to away games, for kit and equipment and referees. This league gets no funding from the professional game yet the professional clubs got to pick up our players without paying any fees. Our league is heavily scouted by League clubs. Work that one out.'

As for the litany of non-League players who have progressed to the Football League and Premier League – how long have you got? Maybe the FA could start by asking the England Under-21 coach, Stuart Pearce, where his career began? There are dozens of players competing in the Football League who started at the grass roots.

So what alternatives to the compensation system might there be? 'I think an open and transparent nature to the registration would be a better approach,' states Huw Jennings, currently academy director at Fulham. 'If a player wants to move they are free to do so, and if a tariff system were to apply so that everybody knew how much it would cost if that boy were to move from one club to another, I think it would help get rid of the underhand practices that undoubtedly exist in certain areas of recruitment.'

Indeed Jennings believes there is too much insecurity around. Instead of being overly protective of their players – like other things in life, if you deny them to someone they will either rebel or, just through inquisitiveness, want to peer over the other side of the fence. 'A few years ago when I was at Southampton, Andrew Surman [at the time of writing a Southampton first-team player] and his family came to me at under-16 level and said, "Andrew would like to look at other clubs. He has never been anywhere else," said his father.

'I spoke to some of the other coaches at our academy who urged me not to allow it because they thought he would end up signing for another club. But my comment was: "Do we have so little faith in what we're doing that a local youngster like Andrew will want to leave the club rather than just having a look elsewhere and then staying?". He is still at Southampton. Sometimes I just think we have to have a little bit more faith.' However, Graham Hawkins at the Football League suggests an alternative idea, 'Don't forget our coaching is free,' he points out. 'The alternative would be for clubs to charge parents for their children to attend centres of excellence or academies.'

Whatever system is put in place, the most important thing is that parents need to be reassured by the football industry that when they bring their children to professional clubs they will be treated in a professional manner and not bought and sold like goods and chattels. The English game needs to find a way out of its current trap. On the one hand it has to offer players the right to choose which club they want to play for – but on the other hand clubs must have the incentive to develop players without losing them unfairly to richer clubs. The influence of agents and avaricious parents has also played its part. Jim Briden at the Football League put his finger firmly on the problem, 'I find the attitude of some parents distasteful when they have been tapped up by a big club and they want the boy to move on. That to me is almost as amoral as the things clubs are perceived to be doing, sometimes their attitude disappoints me.'

Of course, it isn't a perfect world, and football is not always played on a level field either. There is a massive difference between the sort of facilities top Premier League clubs can afford to offer and those found at clubs attempting to provide elite youth development coaching lower down the leagues, where the money is getting tighter.

CHAPTER 7

THE REAL WORLD

It is easy to glide in and out of the superb academies at the likes of Aston Villa, Middlesbrough and Manchester United and think all is well with elite youth development in England.

After all, these clubs are surely the serious players in youth development. They may not necessarily be providing sufficient opportunities for young players, for whatever reason, but their investment is palpable. They have obviously spent the money on their infrastructure – that is clearly visible. According to the Premier League, their member clubs are spending, collectively, on average £40 million a year – that is £2 million per club – to keep their academies fully staffed and operational.

But in the Football League it is a different story. Although 22 Football League clubs have academies (more than the Premier League's 20), 46 of its 72 member clubs have centres of excellence and four don't have either.

Three-quarters of the Football League clubs who responded to research for Richard Lewis's 2007 *Review of Young Player Development in Professional Football* said that the grant funding they receive from the FA and the Premier League, which has been worth £138,000 per season since the programme was devised, is the most important issue to them. In other words, without it, they wouldn't be able to afford to run their academies or centres of excellence at all.

But there is a problem – and it runs right to the heart of the governance of the entire academy system; in exchange for their increased grant aid funds, Football League clubs are being asked to meet Key Performance Indicators (KPIs) and to open up their facilities to independent inspectors.

While it might be frustrating for the FA for the Premier League to choose to prevaricate over outside inspection, matters are far more serious for the Football League, whose impoverished members really do rely on the cash being ladled in their direction.

At present, inspections of club facilities are carried out by the leagues, rather than by outside bodies. But without independence, how can the organisations supplying the funds – the FA and the Premier League – guarantee that the KPIs are being met? Without that guarantee, why should they hand over the money?

Not that you would get this impression from the Football League, who present a bullish front. According to their glossy brochure *Home Grown*, a review of youth development in the Football League published in September 2008, everything in the garden is rosy. 'Ready to set the world alight', is the heraldic opening page headline, with news that the League has secured additional grant aid funds of £3.4 million. Football League chairman Lord Mawhinney is quoted as saying the additional money is 'an endorsement of the work they are doing,' and that it 'demonstrates the strong relationship that exists between the FA and the Football League.' Hmm.

The Football League, he continues is, 'delivering the largest ... development programme for young players in world football.' He goes on, 'We have seen more than 600 young players turn professional in the last four years.' There's more: 'League clubs have played a role in the development of a further 300 senior professionals and youth footballers currently registered with Premier League clubs.' Mawhinney summarises this as, 'a crucial stepping stone to helping English football back to the higher echelons of the world game.' Wow.

'League club investment tops £40 million,' declares an accompanying section – with some £21 million invested by the clubs themselves. But that's playing it down, according to Jim Briden, the League's youth development business manager. 'On average, Football League clubs have contributed about £25 million a year of their own money. Some of this will be in kind. Something like £250 million has been invested since it started.'

'This doesn't include things like investment in facilities,' added Michael Tattersall, the Football League's deputy operating director. 'How do you work out how much is budgeted for youth development and how much is being spent on the first team? It is sometimes very difficult to decide.'

But is it good value for money? 'It must represent good value otherwise our clubs wouldn't do it and we wouldn't have the players to field each weekend,' explains Tattersall. 'If we didn't do it, we would have to bring in foreign players and I don't think our fans would stand for it.'

It all sounds very impressive, but close inspection of the figures reveals a slightly different picture. Some £15 million of the £40 million 'league club investment' is actually the grant funding provided by the FA (£7.8m) and the Premier League (£5.4m) and education funds from the government's Learning and Skills Council for 16- to 18-year-old apprentices. Another sizeable wedge worth £5 million is for players aged between 18 and 21 – but these players are actually senior pros, and the money their wages, rather than 'investment' in youth development.

If you divide up the £25 million that Jim Briden says is being spent between the 68 Football League clubs running academies or centres of excellence, it works out at £367,647 per club. Even allowing for the £1 million budgets of maybe 15 of the better-off Football League clubs, that still leaves a lot of clubs weighing in heavily. If that is the case, why is the grant aid so crucial for 75 per cent of them according to Lewis's research?

Speak to the clubs and you begin to understand why.

Scunthorpe United's Glanford Park is a neatly appointed ground. Built in 1988, just ahead of the post-Taylor Report round of public funding that assisted the rebuilding of Britain's decaying football grounds in the wake of the Hillsborough Disaster, it has few bells and whistles and is a world away from the lavish facilities at the top Premier League clubs.

Youth development manager Tony Daws and his assistant Guy Parkin share a cramped office beneath the main stand. Daws, a former Scunthorpe striker, and Parkin, who played part-time and has a sports science degree, were recruited from Sheffield Wednesday in 2005, having met in 2001 while working for Sheffield United's academy.

They are responsible for developing the club's 108 schoolboy players and 16 full time 16- to 18-year-old apprentices. The annual budget to run their centre of excellence is roughly £300,000 – with more than half of the money coming from the £160,000 they received in grant aid for 2008-09. That figure will increase by £20,000 to £180,000 if they employ a specialist skills coach at £15,000 a year. They will use the remaining £5,000 to part-fund an administrator.

The funding – from both the club's board of directors and the grant aid – is appreciated, but playing in League One, having spent the previous season (2007-08) in the Championship, Scunthorpe are as short of cash as most other clubs at their level. 'We are a small club, but we are enthusiastic about what we do,' said Daws. 'We do what we can within our budget.'

They can't afford full-time youth coaches and the lack of a full-size 3G indoor pitch in North Lincolnshire means they have to ask schoolboy players to schlep over to Hull – some 45 miles away – on cold winter nights so that they can train indoors. However, Parkin says they make up this shortfall by 'being clever,' such as linking up with Hull University. It provides six students to work on collecting data from an innovative player tracking system – a nifty training tool, which tracks the movements and intensity of performance of the players through a device worn on their shorts.

'It costs £28,000 a year,' said Daws, 'we can't afford that, but we provide a small amount and the university covers the rest. It is collaboration. We use their expertise and supply the data for their research.' It allows the club to set individual targets for their players, who are required to keep a diary of the work they put in. 'It moves things on, our data is no longer subjective – the coaches' opinion – it's objective, it's the proof,' explained Daws. 'It means we can actually go to our board of directors and say, "Look at this range of fitness data. This is why we think you should sign him or not."'

'It is out of this world and very advanced,' adds Parkin. 'We have lots of ideas and ways in which we want to push our academy forward. There is a lot of good work going on in youth development, but smaller clubs just don't have the funding.'

Does this lack of money mean that there are clubs that are failing to meet the standards laid in the *Charter for Quality*? 'Loads,' said Parkin, who worryingly added, 'There are a few clubs that we know of, and we cannot mention names, that do not have the required facilities to run an academy, but still have an academy licence and have done so for ten years.'

What about the 46 centres of excellence at Football League clubs? 'You will find that 95 per cent of clubs with centres of excellence don't have their own training ground,' said Daws. 'They use school facilities or use whatever they can'.

'Centres of excellence are considered to be elite development but they're not being taught in elite facilities,' said Parkin. 'There are a lot of them whose facilities are no better than junior teams.'

'In fact, some junior team will have better facilities,' added Daws.

This isn't against the *Charter for Quality* regulations, and it can be unfair to pick on cash-strapped clubs – but it isn't what you expect from elite youth development. During visits to professional academies and centres of excellence down the years I have seen matches played at schools and colleges, players eating their lunchtime meals while sat on the floor in the reception area of a local college and a former Premier League club whose training ground was at a works sports ground.

Daws and Parkin insist that many of the youth programmes they know rely solely on grant aid. They thought some clubs contributed an extra £50,000 or £100,000 from their own coffers, and others spent up to £500,000. It isn't lack of will – just a lack of cash in the game at this level.

'It is frustrating because you see the money being spent in the Premier League on players' wages and for a fraction of that we could build permanent facilities that would help develop players for the foreseeable future,' said Daws.

However, their frustration is exacerbated by the fact that the results of the Football League's inspections don't reach the wider public.

'There is nothing that distinguishes the good youth programmes from the poor ones,' said Daws. 'We believe we are running a programme here that is one of the best in the country, but there is no information for parents to access and use to make a decision.'

'We are audited on an annual basis by the Football League,' explained Parkin. 'Then they write a report about us. Last time, we got a glowing reference because of the things we are trying to do. But nobody sees that report apart from the Football League – parents don't get access to that because it is not made public.'

This is something that Michael Tattersall, deputy operations director at the Football League, is keen to push forward and is a suggestion he made at the Professional Game Youth Development Group, an organisation set up to deal with the recommendations of the *Lewis Report*. As ever with football, politics is getting in the way. 'I proposed a football version of Ofsted, an independent standards unit which would monitor the clubs and provide the information publicly,' insisted Tattersall. 'We are all for that. We don't have anything to hide. I proposed it and didn't find any support. No takers. The feeling I got was they don't necessarily accept recommendations from the Football League ... but we haven't given up on the idea – in fact we have come up with further proposals for an independent standards unit to assess clubs in the Football and Premier Leagues.'

But how independent should independent be? There is disagreement among the three main governing bodies in English football – the FA, the Premier League and the Football League – about who should actually carry out the inspections, and scepticism, not least of all as I heard in Scunthorpe, among the clubs themselves.

Have any clubs lost their licences for any reason? 'One club did, and that was partly to do with financial irregularities in the grant aid funding, and a few have been threatened with it,' said Jim Briden. 'Although we don't publicly name clubs, we don't sweep it under the carpet either. We compile an annual report and that is sent to the FA as one of the funding partners of the programme.'

'We drive standards up,' insisted Graham Hawkins, the Football League's head of player development. 'It's not just a matter of ticking boxes. We try to pass on information and shared good practice. It is more than just getting a licence.'

It would be easy to criticise clubs for appearing to fail to invest in youth development – how on earth do they expect to develop players if they don't spend some money? However, the financial disparities between the Premier League and the Football League are enormous. There are many figures that support this fact – but the most important is TV revenue.

Days after West Bromwich Albion had been promoted to the Premier League from the Championship in May 2008 for the third time in six seasons, the club's chairman, Jeremy Peace, explained the difference having TV rights would make to their income. The Baggies would be lucky to muster £2 million a year in the Championship. In the Premier League they are guaranteed at least £30 million – with a raft of other easily accrued commercial spin-offs that can readily bump that up to £60 million. Stay there, and year-on-year, it means the gap widens to a chasm, with clubs competing in the Champions League racing off into a different financial stratosphere.

It is possible to come plummeting back down of course. Leeds United, in League One at the time of writing, are paying the price for infamously 'living the dream'. Many other clubs have borrowed and gambled in a desperate, sometimes overly optimistic, bid to rough it among the English football's big boys, many of them laden with debt and in hock to multinational owners, who, should they decide to sell up or pull the plug (and why not in these perilous financial times?), could plunge them into deep crisis. Few clubs are safe.

It is among former Premier League clubs where most of the Football League academy licences have been awarded. The likes of Leicester City, Coventry City, Southampton, Charlton, Crystal Palace, Norwich City, Ipswich Town, Wolves, Birmingham City, Derby County, Nottingham Forest, both Sheffield clubs and, of course, Leeds (who are having to lease back the superb training ground they developed at Thorpe Arch) built their facilities in more prosperous times. For some, this investment has come to their rescue.

In 2003, Derby County – relegated from the Premier League and struggling with crippling debt – appointed George Burley as their manager. Burley's faith in youth players had been established at Ipswich Town and, under his watchful eye, Derby regularly fielded five or six academy players in their team.

The undoubted star was Tom Huddlestone, an England youth midfielder who was thrown into the first team at 17 years old and clocked up 88 appearances before being sold to Tottenham Hotspur in 2005 for £2.5 million. Other players blooded by Burley included 16 year olds Nathan Doyle and Lee Holmes, and under 19 year olds Lee Camp, Lee Grant, Pablo Mills and Marcus Tudgay.

Speaking at the time Burley's attitude was refreshingly simple, 'If they are good enough they're old enough,' he said. 'You've got to have the courage to put them in – and make sure the path from academy to reserves to the first team is really tight.'

Terry Westley, Derby's academy director at the time – he is now at Birmingham City – said the inspirational effect among the academy players was palpable. 'The younger boys get a lift when they see older academy players getting their chance. It's good for the staff too – it makes you feel worthwhile.'

Derby survived and thrived – reaching the Championship play-offs in 2005 before Burley departed.

Traditionally, youth development has been one way smaller clubs have balanced their books. They have sold on their better, or at least more valuable, players (hopefully home-grown and cheaply acquired), and have then punted up the leagues. However, this option has ground to a halt in the academy years. In fact, it has reversed. The big clubs are now acquiring their players at junior age levels (and remember, it is now a process that starts at nine years of age) so although some of the fees may seem relatively high for players whose futures are far from guaranteed, they nonetheless have potentially successful players signed up before they reach senior level, when more significant money is paid for the transfer of players. Add the increasing option of buying over-seas players and it makes it even harder for small clubs to sell upwards.

With their massive squads and huge financial muscle the top clubs can carry an enormous number of professional players on their books. They therefore look to loan their players out to get first-team experience, and it is cheaper for many Football League clubs to field a few loan players, sharing the wages with the club loaning the player out, rather than have their own players on long-term deals that eat into their budgets.

Midway through the 2008-09 season, Liverpool had 15 players out on loan, Arsenal 12, Manchester United, 11 and Chelsea, 10 – most to Football League clubs. At the same point among the bottom four clubs in League Two, Grimsby had eight players in on loan, Luton had seven, Barnet five and Bournemouth four.

In terms of transfers upwards, during the summer of 2008 Keith Andrews, who went from MK Dons to Blackburn Rovers for £1.3 million (where he joined former Dons manager Paul Ince) was the only player to move from Leagues One or Two to the Premier League. Several players moved from Championship clubs to the Premier League, however most of these were players jumping straight back into the league from relegated teams. The only significant piece of business in the January 2009 window was Jamie Ward moving from Chesterfield to Sheffield United for £330,000.

This is no anomaly. Back in 2000-01 there were no player movements from the old Division Three (now League Two) to the Premier League and just three from Division Two (now League One) worth £3.27 million, and £46.5 million worth of players from the old Division One (now the Championship). By far the biggest trade for smaller clubs was, as it is today, among clubs at their own level.

With a shrinking market upwards, transfer sales from the Premier League downwards have increased. It was worth £22 million in 2001-02, and just short of £25 million in 2008-09, although now most player movements are loans, often on a season-long basis.

Despite the difficulties of selling players upwards, Football League clubs are offering their home-grown players more openings than Premier League clubs. The lack of available cash may even be helping. The Football League's *Home Grown* brochure says that 600 players have signed professional contracts in the past four seasons. Youth development can also prove to be a valuable route to long-term success.

In 2004 I visited one of the notable success stories in English youth development at Crewe Alexandra. 'Reputation is everything in youth development,' said Dario Gradi, the man who has masterminded Crewe's remarkable record in unearthing raw diamonds, polishing them, playing them in the first team and selling some of them on for a handsome profit to clubs who know they are getting value for money in securing a Gradi-developed player. The proceeds are then ploughed back to develop more players. It is something Gradi has done at Crewe since 1983, spending most of that time as manager, and more recently as Crewe's technical director.

They don't waste money on frills and fancies at Crewe. There is no elegant facade or swanky reception, no huge pot plants and circular tables with an array of football industry magazines draped across them. We met in the club canteen. Gradi breezed in full of apologies for his lateness (I had watched him schooling some players on a pitch) and explained in detail how the club's ethos has developed and grown. It has not only enabled Crewe to stay financially afloat, but has seen them rise from perennial strugglers in the old Fourth Division to a Championship-level team for eight seasons (between 1997 and 2006, with one relegation and promotion back in between). For a town with a population of just 67,000 people, sandwiched between the football hotbeds of the north-west and the Potteries, it is even more remarkable.

Warm, intelligent, but quietly spoken, Gradi explained that, 'what we have here cannot easily be copied. It takes time and patience to develop these ethics. Most clubs don't operate on the kind of long-term basis you need.'

A list of Crewe's alumni makes impressive reading. In the 1980s their early successes included Rob Jones, Geoff Thomas and David Platt. The 1990s graduate stars were Craig Hignett, Robbie Savage, Danny Murphy, Neil Lennon and Seth Johnson. In the 2000s England striker Dean Ashton's move to Norwich for £3 million set a new Crewe transfer record, with the sales of Rob Hulse to West Bromwich, Luke Varney to Charlton Athletic and Billy Jones to Preston North End also raising substantial funds.

There is also the invaluable contribution their academy players have made to the club's first team down the years. Currently half of their first-team squad is home-grown. While that would be a proud boast for many clubs, at Crewe it is actually quite disappointing.

At the time of my visit, 28 of their 32 senior players had been produced by the academy.

It initially cost Crewe £2 million to develop their training ground at Rease Heath. They spent their money on essentials to match the best clubs in youth development – such as an £800,000 indoor centre.

At their peak Crewe looked to get four players a season from the academy into the first-team squad. 'Most clubs would be happy to get one or two through,' Gradi explained. Former players and their parents usually stay in touch. 'You need to build a relationship of trust with parents, these aren't things you need to have as a rule – they are common sense,' before pausing to chuckle. 'But football doesn't always work like that.'

But very few other cash-strapped clubs have followed Crewe's lead – looking instead for a short-term fix rather than long-term vision. Some even fail to invest in youth development coaching staff, making attempts to recruit on the cheap. One former coach, who has been involved at all levels of the game from the Premier League down, revealed just how cheap. He has pretty much left the game, but had been asked to coach at Football League centres of excellence. When he asked how much he would be paid he was told, '£25 each for two sessions a week and a match on Sunday,' – £75 in total. No petrol expenses. It wasn't hard to say no. 'All the clubs in this region offer pretty much the same,' he said, before mentioning a list of clubs from Championship to League Two level.

At the sharp end of the Football League these are the terms and conditions coaches are being hired on. Small wonder many coaches have vacated the game in preference to opportunities elsewhere – such as the burgeoning college sector, overseas or early retirement.

Huw Jennings, the former head of youth development at the Premier League, was amazed to discover that a club promoted to England's top flight from the Championship – rather than viewing the feast of lolly about to come their way as a chance to invest in their academy – actually faced a reduced budget because they had lost their grant subsidy. 'It was a disappointment to me,' said Jennings. 'I would like to see the Premier League board be stronger in maintaining the quality standards of all its clubs in this area.'

For all the puffed up self-importance at the top end of the game, *Home Grown* emphasises the significant contribution players developed in the Football League are making to England's national squads: there are 48 per cent playing in England's senior team, 44 per cent at under-21 level, 50 per cent at under-19, and a whopping 75 per cent at under-18. These figures suggest that Football League clubs are good at developing quality players despite the obvious financial difficulties – more than half of Football League clubs have been in administration at some point since the advent of the Premier League.

Some observers, like Howard Wilkinson, dismiss this as a sign of the weakness of the senior England team. Others think that home-grown players need a helping hand to reach the top level. For some, this means the introduction of quotas. In December 2008 at an extraordinary general meeting held at Derby County's Pride Park, a majority of Football League clubs voted in favour of introducing a policy from season 2009-10 that will require four players in a 16-man matchday squad to have been registered domestically for at least three years before their 21st birthday.

An overall majority vote, including a majority of Championship clubs, gave the proposal the green light. A player is deemed 'home-grown' if he is registered for three entire seasons (or 36 months) prior to turning 21 with a club affiliated to the Football Association or the Football Association of Wales. 'If it can give players more opportunity, then it has to be worthwhile,' said Graham Hawkins of the Football League. 'It has ensured we have some players in these teams. I would like to see the number increased, but I am sure that will come.'

The proposal is in line with the approach favoured by UEFA, rather than the 'six plus five' approach proposed by world governing body FIFA, which stipulates that six of a team's starting XI should be eligible to play for the national team of the country of the club. The Football League executive had concerns over the legality of the latter in European law and the employment rights of EU citizens. This means that players will be considered 'home-grown' regardless of their nationality.

Premier League clubs look likely to follow the lead of the Football League with the home-grown issue due for discussion at the League's

2009 summer meeting. 'Our clubs have asked us to set out the arguments to improve opportunities for home-grown players,' confirmed Mike Foster, general secretary of the Premier League. Though he added a note of caution, 'Whether or not they wish to take the idea forward as the Football League have remains to be seen. I think we need to improve the quality of players. It would increase the number of home-grown players – but would it raise the standard? I'm not convinced.'

However, a bigger threat looms large over the future of Football League's youth development programme. In his 2007 review Richard Lewis offered 64 recommendations to point the way ahead for English youth development – the first major shake-up since Howard Wilkinson's *A Charter for Quality* ten years earlier.

Lewis, who had been brought in essentially to sort out wrangles between the three main football governing bodies in England – The FA, The Premier League and the Football League – reported, 'During the review I came across many examples of best practice and a strong desire for continuous improvement. My report seeks to build upon the good work that is taking place and to give the football authorities a framework on which to build.

'I was very pleased that at a recent meeting during which I presented the report all three organisations supported the review overall and committed to implementing an action plan. I am confident the vast majority of the recommendations that I have made will be agreed by all parties and I believe the basis is there for real sustained progress in the development of young professional players.'

His key findings are covered in detail in the next chapter; however, two important issues were particularly pertinent to the Football League and its member clubs, especially those in Leagues One and Two.

Lewis's report highlighted the fact that Football League clubs, 'need stability and consistency of funding' and he recommended an increase in the annual youth development grant aid provided by The FA and Premier League to the Football League clubs, which had been stuck at the same level – £138,000 per club – for ten years. Lewis argued that if raised in line with the Retail Price Index this should be worth £180,000. The grant was subsequently raised to this level in 2008-09.

It had been a wound that had been allowed to fester and was one of many reasons that cash-strapped Football League clubs were slipping further behind the richer Premier League clubs.

But the increased grant aid wasn't to be doled out willy-nilly. Lewis wanted Key Performance Indicators (KPIs) to be met – and for the increased funds to 'target specific activities and only given to individual clubs to reward best practice'.

Key Performance Indicators are financial and non-financial calculations used to help an organisation define and measure progress toward goals. They can be delivered through business techniques to assess the present state of the business and to assist in prescribing a course of action. KPIs are frequently used to 'value' difficult-to-measure activities such as the benefits of leadership development, engagement, service and satisfaction.

Lewis also wanted to establish quality assurance measurements based on International Standards of Organisation (ISOs) to underpin the monitoring standards. He insisted that failing academies and centres of excellence should face suspension, downgrading or the withdrawal of licences should they fail to meet these standards.

Grateful to receive the money – many Football League clubs would have to fold their youth programmes without it – an important question remained. Who would ensure that KPIs were being met? At the moment, as discussed, responsibility for inspections rest with the leagues – the Premier League for its member clubs and the Football League for its 72 clubs. But the FA has increasingly stated its desire to be involved in inspection procedures to ensure that the money it is giving to Football League academies and centre of excellences is being spent to drive up standards and to meet the terms under which they are granting licences in the first place.

However, in January 2009, the body created to drive through the Lewis recommendations – the Professional Game Youth Development Group – chaired by Howard Wilkinson, the architect of the academy and centre of excellence system, fell apart amid acrimony. These issues are also discussed in the next chapter, but the current impasse leaves the Football League and its member clubs in the most vulnerable position of the three main parties. They need their funding partners to have confidence in their inspection regimes. The call for an independent report, provided ultimately by Richard Lewis, occurred after the FA and the leagues went out jointly to inspect a number of clubs together in 2005 and came back with similar conclusions as to how to move forward.

This is how Sir Trevor Brooking, the FA head of development, recalled events, 'We went out with two Football League representatives of the monitoring unit, two Premier League inspectors and two of my national coaches, to have a look at some of the more contentious clubs. We identified three Premier League clubs and three Football League clubs that we wanted to put on notice to give them the rest of the season, six to eight months, to make some necessary improvements. Unfortunately, though, when the Premier League and Football League Boards heard this they informed the FA's Technical Control Board that in their view the FA no longer had responsibility or control of Academies and Centres of Excellence. In the future the Football League would regulate their clubs and the Premier League sanctioned their clubs. In other words it was like the two league bodies marking their own exam papers, which I did not believe was a structure that would maintain the necessary standards in coaching and player development.'

Lewis was asked to provide an overview, and although the three bodies have sat around the table, they have still not been able to agree.

Although he accepts calls for an independent standards unit, Michael Tattersall does not believe that the Football League should have to concede authority of inspections to the FA: 'The FA is the governing body of football, but that doesn't mean it does everything. The leagues have their own competence and we do it in partnership with the FA. Monitoring of centres and academies is carried out under the umbrella regulations of the FA rules, which say that clubs should be monitored and it's for the leagues to licence the clubs. I don't see any issue with that.'

However, while the Premier League could, in theory at least, cut loose and withdraw its funding obligations to the rest of the game and go it alone, the Football League cannot afford to divorce itself in this way. The Premier League, remember, has done it already when it split away from the collectivist Football League structure to negotiate its own commercial contracts, in particular increasingly lucrative TV deals.

'There is a danger that if we take a 92-club approach that we will go at the pace of the slowest,' warns Mike Foster, general secretary of the Premier League. 'It would be easy for us to say "thanks a lot Football League, thanks a lot FA, we're going to do it on our own". We haven't chosen to do that. We could do things a lot quicker because we wouldn't have to agree with other people – we would be our own masters. But I think the FA is the competent body to deliver coaching development and although the Football League clubs don't have as much money as our clubs, they are great breeding grounds for young talent which our clubs might be able to use in the future, so we are prepared to work with them.'

Small wonder that the Football League, which receives £5.4 million each year from the Premier League for youth development, doesn't want to pick a fight, 'We haven't disagreed with any proposals,' said Michael Tattersall. 'We are eager to make progress. The Premier League invests £5.4 million a year in the Football League Trust for youth development grant aid – which is a sizeable contribution to what we do. In return, our clubs develop a lot of players that will be able to play at Football League level and some ultimately at Premier League level. We have a good relationship with the Premier League. If there is something they are saying about us holding them back I would like to know what it is because we want to push ahead to improve things too.'

The battle between the three main football bodies remains a turf war – with each jumping up to take occasional potshots at the other. However, this war of attrition involves staking out ground for a system involving the lives of the 10,000 boys registered with clubs each season and represents arguably the strongest link between football clubs and their communities – surely the fans, players and parents deserve better of the game's governors than this endless politicking?

Apparently not.

CHAPTER 8

POLITICAL FOOTBALL

If all was totally rosy you would not be reading this report,
which would have had no need to have been commissioned.
Richard Lewis, *A Review of Young Player Development in Professional*
Football, 2007

By the time Howard Wilkinson left his job after five-and-a-half years
as FA technical director in October 2002 to have a final stab at top-
flight football management at Sunderland, his call for 'quality and
unity' in the *Charter for Quality* had already hit the buffers. Not for
the first time – in fact, a theme running throughout its history –
English football's governing bodies seemed to decide that bickering
was more important than the greater good of the sport. Their duty in
this case was to make sure that a new elite youth development
programme – one that was granting far greater powers to football
clubs in terms of coaching children with an inevitable impact on their
education and child welfare – was working correctly.

Yet none of the main rules and regulations outlined in Wilkinson's
charter were significantly developed or changed in the ten years since
it had been published until Richard Lewis's review of young player
development in 2007. Had football's main three governing bodies –
the FA, Premier League and Football League – thought they were all
doing such a stunningly successful job that no fine tuning had been
necessary? Didn't they realise that this new system would have to
adapt to meet every challenge it faced?

In actual fact the *Lewis Report* – detailed though it was and ultimately offering 64 recommendations to improve youth development in England to pave a new way forward – had not been commissioned with that in mind. Lewis had not been called in to assess, protect or enshrine the rights and interests of the 10,000 boys playing in or registered with academies or centres of excellence, nor the thousands more youngsters in development centres who were being trawled for, 'culled', bought and sold. Nor was he called in because of concerns about the welfare or education of the boys or to re-assess the quality of coaching and whether it was working in 'the best interests' of the players – something that Wilkinson's charter was at pains to point out. It wasn't even because England's national teams were not winning things at any level and were copping lots of media stick.

It was because the three governing groups had got bored with spattering the walls of Soho Square with the jelly and trifle they hurled at each other during meetings of the Technical Control Board, the body that deals with youth development. Jointly they decided to call for a fresh pair of eyes, an independent advisor, to appraise the situation. It was for their benefit – not the boys or the parents doing the thrice-weekly academy run, or schoolteachers spotting kids creeping into school yawning, nor to protect the significant sums of public money pouring into the youth programmes or education budgets. It was to resolve their own organisational issues.

Richard Lewis is executive chairman of the Rugby Football League and a former Davis Cup tennis player. His direct involvement in the football industry was zilch. Like Lord Justice Taylor – who had no specific football background when he was asked to make sense of the causes of the Hillsborough Disaster when 96 football fans lost their lives and to tell the football industry how to make its stadiums safe – this made Lewis ideal for the job. It needed someone in a position to be able to stand back and assess the wider picture.

During the review process, Lewis attempted to get the various parties to recognise an important thing, which they had long forgotten among the infighting; that they actually agreed on many more things than they disagreed. 'A great deal has been done,' said Lewis, 'however, work needs to be done to build on the progress already achieved.'

'Richard Lewis was an excellent chairman. He was very good at listening and drawing conclusions,' recalls Michael Tattersall of the Football League, who worked on the review group. 'It was a step forward. It demonstrated, above all else, that we need to work with each other.'

With the clear aim to resolve the squabbling, plus a time limit to produce both an interim report and a final one, Lewis's focus was essentially narrow. Notably absent from the list of Lewis's discussions and consultations are any meetings with parents and players. It is not difficult, as I have discovered, to find people who are disgruntled with the way they have been treated by clubs or have problems with varying elements of the youth development system. Lewis's review, therefore, is only a partial picture, a view that he readily acknowledged. 'It [the review] does not go into great detail on every aspect of football academies and centres of excellence … this will disappoint some people who are under the impression that this review will pronounce judgement on the minutiae of the programme.'

Nonetheless Lewis provided a commanding overview – a state of play if you like – that offered no less than 64 separate recommendations (including an increase in the annual grant fund paid to Football League clubs, raised from £138,000 to £180,000 in line with the Retail Price Index already discussed) that he felt could improve youth development in England.

From the outset he reiterated Wilkinson's belief, presented in the *Charter for Quality*, that a 'player-focussed approach' was needed, highlighting in bold lettering that 'the development of the individual', rather than the culture of the team, 'is paramount'. He added, 'If football in England wishes to be the very best in the world it must be the best at young player development,' which should be centred on a 'culture of excellence'.

His recommendations included a raft of changes great and small – many the sort of essential fettling you might have reasonably expected as the academy system chugged into gear. Some were structural, such as maintaining the dual system of academies and centres of excellence (though he suggested they might be re-branded).

Lewis came down against the implementation of quotas as a means of increasing opportunities for home-grown players preferring, 'full support and investment to be given in the drive to improve the quality of coaching at the youngest age groups'. Tossing the ball into the FA's court, he wanted a core national coaching syllabus to improve the quality of coaching with 'a clear strategy and business plan for the development of coach education'.

Remarkably, it hadn't produced one – even though the academy system had been hobbling along for ten years. In fact there were no age-specific coaching qualifications available. Neither was there enough help for inexperienced academy staff, (Lewis suggested a mentoring system to help younger academy coaches) and enough Continuous Personal Development (CPD) courses available regionally.

This beggared belief – what had the FA been up to during the ten years since producing the *Charter for Quality*?

In setting the FA this task, Lewis had accepted one of Sir Trevor Brooking's long-held mantras that the skill level of the country's 5- to 11-year-old players simply wasn't good enough – that for all the clubs' trawling, sifting and culling, better quality coaching was needed at the youngest age levels. Lewis also agreed that licensing had to be considered for the pre-academy development centres that had mushroomed fairly free of regulation and responsibility. He saw the National Football Centre – Howard Wilkinson's dream nerve centre for coaching, which lay half built at Burton-upon-Trent – as a venue to be considered for a national base to deliver education courses to coaches.

He wanted more flexibility built into the academy and centre of excellence games programme to reduce the amount of travelling for players and parents and to limit the number of mandatory games – something which had been called for but, again, had been largely ignored as the Technical Liaison Group opted instead to coat the walls of Soho Square with fresh layers of jelly and ice cream.

To help the development of young players, Lewis wanted the parties to consider introducing a club-based, under-21 match programme – and to have specific directors or senior executives at boardroom level at each club with responsibility for youth development matters. They would be trained and well-versed in the relevant issues.

One more contentious idea – which appeared to be there to appease the 'predatory' clubs – was to allow registered scouts to watch any academy and centre of excellence matches they chose. Some clubs had prevented scouts attending their matches after losing players to the same rival clubs over and over again.

To counter this proposal, Lewis also wanted tariffs to be considered so that compensation payments could be set when players moved between clubs, and for the system to be 'transparent', with the payments published – something, he said, that should stop bigger clubs snapping up smaller clubs' best players on the cheap.

On the release of players, Lewis wanted assessment trials (currently only offered to boys aged 18) to be extended to other age groups, and for better and more flexible relationships to be formed between schools and clubs in order for players to be released from schools to train with clubs either during school time or immediately afterwards.

On coaching qualifications, 'a particularly thorny issue' noted Lewis, he was clearly exacerbated to discover that it had become accepted industry practice for coaches to be given an 18-month dispensation to obtain the relevant qualifications after getting the job. As he observed, this had been a transitionary measure designed to help smooth things over during the opening of academies and centres of excellence. It hadn't been intended as a permanent rule. 'The automatic dispensation period for the acquisition of coaching qualifications should be removed,' said Lewis. 'Coaches must be qualified to do the job from day one.' Amazingly, clubs had thought it OK to employ unqualified staff to coach children.

On leadership and coordination (the main issue which Lewis was brought in to resolve), he described the present structure as, 'at best cumbersome and unclear'. He stated, 'It is not my intention to stray into areas of broader governance and control, yet in the specific areas of young player development it is evident that clearer lines of responsibility and accountability would serve to improve quality.'

In sum total, Lewis's report delivered a carefully worded attack on the way the various bodies in charge of youth development had failed to deal with issues as they had arisen while the system had bedded in.

In order to get his recommendations implemented he made a specific plea, 'I urge the Football Association, the Football League and the Premier League to work together to ensure rapid progress.' He thought a streamlined executive group would work best. 'In my experience,' wrote Lewis, 'small, executive-led groups can make speedy operational decisions where lager bodies of representatives often find it more difficult.' In particular, he suggested the formation of a Youth Management Group (YMG), comprised of equal representatives from each of the FA, the Premier League and the Football League, managed by an independent chairman.

When it was published in July 2007, the official response to Lewis's report from each of the main three governing bodies was warm. The FA's chief executive at the time, Brian Barwick, thanked Lewis for his 'excellent work.' He continued, 'Youth development is integral to the long-term health and success of the English game and it was important to bring in someone with sports experience but with an outside perspective.' Barwick said the FA would 'take the summer' to assess his recommendations in more detail. There was, he insisted, 'broad agreement' between the FA and the two leagues on the best way forward. Premier League chief executive Richard Scudamore was also in a thoughtful mood, 'We will now take time to reflect on its findings before deciding the best way forward to ensure youth development is resourced and prioritised appropriately and effectively.'

Andy Williamson, the Football League's chief operating officer, was even more forthcoming, 'This report will help define the way forward for youth development in professional football,' he said. 'Supporters at all levels of the game want to see their club developing their own playing talent and for Football League clubs it offers a framework that secures the future of their youth schemes and enables them to continue identifying, training and educating the professional players of tomorrow.'

The signs looked good that all parties would fold away their party hats, put the streamers in the bin and get on with the many and varied aspects of implementation. Mike Foster, at the Premier League, favoured a full implementation of Lewis's recommendations.

'Because of the political infighting, we wanted to implement the Lewis recommendations 100 per cent. We thought it was a good piece of work and we were prepared to adopt it wholesale.'

Great – although there was one problem: 'But the stakeholders wouldn't accept that'.

'We thought it was very positive,' said Michael Tattersall at the Football League. 'It was very productive. We have issues with a couple of things. One is scouting – he recommended open access for scouts, which we think is a recipe for unsettling players. That said, we want to improve the training of scouts. We also think a tariff for compensation isn't suitable. It just doesn't make sense because some players may not be worth the fee quoted and others may be worth a lot more. But it would be wrong to focus on those two issues because on the whole it is a way forward.'

But it all started to go wrong as soon as they sat around the table again. With the FA's Technical Control Board in the sidings, the new body that Lewis's report had called the Youth Management Group was actually constituted as the Professional Game Youth Development Group (PGYDG), which had the task of implementing Lewis's recommendations and plotting an onward course for English youth development.

From the outset Sir Trevor Brooking, the FA's head of development, was not overly optimistic. 'My concern was that the new body was made up of the three stakeholders, the FA and the two leagues, which just meant the governing body would get out-voted all the time by the leagues ... I wanted the League Managers Association (LMA), the PFA and the FA Coaches Association (FACA) on board too, so six groups would make decisions about what was best for player development. I was concerned that the leagues would only really look at it from the club-owners point of view.'

Bizarrely, that meant that the FA was actually arguing for less control of its national youth development policy, not more. 'We are the only governing body that doesn't have power over its academy system,' admitted Brooking ironically. 'The other thing that Lewis recommended was that the people on the new group should be technical people – well, they aren't.'

In his review Lewis laid out the credentials of the person he thought should lead the new management group, 'It should be independently chaired by someone with a strong football background'. The person selected was none other than Howard Wilkinson – architect of the academy and centre of excellence system. 'It was a bit like asking Sir Christopher Wren to come back and rebuild St Paul's Cathedral,' joked one interviewee.

Wilkinson had been critical of the way clubs had implemented the *Charter for Quality* – so he was under suspicion from the start – but was nonetheless seen as an expert in the field and, as chairman of the LMA, brought another key stakeholder to the table.

The PGYDG initially consisted of Wilkinson, three FA representatives in Brooking, John Peacock (head of coaching) and national coach Steve Wigley; the Premier League had Liverpool chief executive Rick Parry, Damien Comolli, director of football at Tottenham Hotspur, and Huw Jennings, its head of youth development at the table; while the Football League offered two administrators, deputy operations director Michael Tattersall, Sheffield United director Terry Robinson plus its head of player development Graham Hawkins. The first meeting was held in April 2008 – with England manager Fabio Capello, keen to show his support for the new venture, attending the first couple of meetings.

The problem was that the simmering tensions that existed prior to Lewis's report would not go away, even though the actual divisive issues, as Lewis suggested, were not numerous. The club versus country row clung in the air, as ever. However, the main sticking points were on the one hand monitoring and inspections – the FA wanted, not unreasonably on the face of it, some input into the assessment of academies and centres of excellence that are licensed in their name – and on the other hand the leagues preferred to see the FA busy itself with designing and delivering new coach education courses for its academy staff.

'Accepting recommendations and driving them through are two different things,' admitted Brooking. 'There is a lot of positivity out there. But we've got to get the decision makers to be comfortable with quality assurances and KPIs. There are some really good clubs that are doing some excellent work and they are actually annoyed with the group because we are not implementing the Lewis recommendations.'

However, the leagues, while accepting a broader church should be involved in monitoring the standards at clubs, would not accept the FA's claim that, as the governing body of the sport and one of the funding agencies for Football League programmes – providing £7.8m annually – it should be involved in inspections. 'The money is distributed by the Football League Trust – and the FA has given their money to the trust for them to distribute,' argued Brooking. 'But that is without the quality assurances in place because the PGYDG cannot agree on who should inspect the clubs.'

The leagues insisted they have nothing to hide and are not out to protect any member clubs failing to meet the licensing criteria – but Mike Foster of the Premier League certainly doesn't want the FA in charge of monitoring his member clubs' facilities. 'The FA has always been eager to take responsibility for monitoring,' he said. 'They seem to want to have control of everything that goes on in academies. The FA pay, as we do, a significant sum of money (£5.4m) to Football League youth development centres, so I think they are entitled to check how that money is being spent. They don't, however, pay a penny towards Premier League academies and I don't think the FA is any better placed than we are to assess Premier League academies. I think an independent group would do it better because they have no allegiances.'

The Football League was particularly concerned that unsympathetic assessors would look closely at the centres of excellence at small clubs. 'Monitoring is carried out by the leagues,' said Michael Tattersall. 'We want our clubs to succeed. We will monitor them to a strict regime, but we don't want them to give up. If there is something that needs to be addressed we want them to address it and improve.'

All sides seemed to agree that an independent standards unit is the way forward – and that the data it produces should be available in the public domain, but if they cannot sit around a table to discuss these issues how will they ever hope to appoint a panel they deem acceptable to carry out the work? 'We have put together a document between the Football League, the FA and ourselves, that still needs fine tuning but which we hope will soon be ready to go out to tender,' said Mike Foster. 'It is a huge piece of work and it demonstrates that the leagues are prepared to be accountable.'

But differences in opinion remain about the actual role of the FA in all of this. 'The FA's job is to lead coach education,' insisted Graham Hawkins, head of player development at the Football League. While Huw Jennings, former head of youth development at the Premier League, said, 'The FA has to recognise it is part of a pluralist society. It sees itself as the governing body that is therefore in control, but its obsession with control masks its ability to contribute. There are people at the FA who insist they want to work alongside clubs, but show me where they have demonstrated that in action?

'It is very clear the leagues have the power to licence, they have the autonomy to register the players. While the FA's programme of excellence sits on top of the league rules, the reality is that de facto power is with the leagues. The FA is moaning about the lack of independence because it is working in a tripartite fashion with the leagues. But it won't be a one-third stakeholder. It wants to be a greater stakeholder and I'm not sure that is feasible.'

While the politics surrounding youth development rumble on, there are questions of public confidence and accountability that go unanswered. These are questions that I have asked many times over the years. Have any clubs had academy or centre of excellence licenses revoked? If so, which ones, when, and for what reason(s)?

Names are never mentioned – yet even in the Premier League some club academies are apparently not up to scratch, 'I'm not going to mention names, but our board receives regular monitoring reports on each club,' said Mike Foster. 'At the end of 2007-08 we had issues with one club. Before that, we had issues with a handful of clubs who weren't meeting the standards. We gave them a deadline of getting up to standard and those clubs have now done so.'

What issues were they failing on? 'Facilities, primarily'. With all the money sloshing around surely they could afford to spend the money on facilities? 'They obviously needed a bit more encouragement,' he said.

Of course, these questions are of primary importance to parents who want information to help them to decide where to send their sons, information that is widely available in other areas of education. It's important not to forget that, in the case of 16- to 18-year-old apprentices, football offers two types of education – football and academic. The commitment is full time.

Not to be able to get answers from a sport that plays its business out so readily in the public eye seems odd. After all, why should a sport whose clubs are judged by league tables actually object to them for the performance of football academies? How can parents decide whether to send their child to an academy or centre of excellence (often committing, including travel time, the sort of hours that could be classified as part-time employment) unless they have a visible benchmark on how well it is performing?

As things stand, they have two choices, 'The luck of the draw and basing their opinion on the individuals they meet,' said Brooking. 'There are some really good ones, but there are others which aren't. Some people do come to us and ask for advice, which we cannot give because we have no direct input or direct access to any of the work going on other than running courses and talking to their [the clubs] staff.

'I get terribly frustrated,' continued Brooking. 'Because I can't deliver the sort of things other governing bodies in other countries can. I think it is wrong – I have said it is wrong but you get battered for saying these things. All I can do is voice the concerns of the people I meet at clubs who work in a system they think is flawed. They want it to be changed but you cannot get the decision-making process to do that. It is unsatisfactory. I am trying to support it. I am trying to be a good football person. The game is awash with money and the governing body is saying we want to ring-fence some of it to develop our own young players.

'This is about the quality of our youngsters. There are more players coming from abroad. They are filling up our first teams and they are filling up our academies. Soon they will start to fill up Football League clubs unless we raise the quality of our youngsters.'

But that is not how the leagues see it. They would prefer the FA to concentrate on coach education – in particular age-specific, youth development coaching qualifications, which, bizarrely, are only being developed some ten years after the FA designed a system to allow clubs to coach under nines. 'The FA needs to work alongside its partners in the game and stop telling them what to do. It needs to demonstrate its leadership in coach education, which is one of its primary functions, instead of saying it is in charge of player development,' said Huw Jennings. 'The FA is not in charge of player development. Players spend their time with the clubs and could maybe spend some time with the FA to get additional experiences, which for some players may be great, but they should stop telling people they are in control of player development, because they're not.

'The FA is suffering from people in the upper echelons not understanding what its needs are and not promoting itself effectively within its own organisation to secure the resources it needs to succeed.'

'You need to ask the FA where they are with producing a coaching manual,' said Michael Tattersall. 'Why hasn't the FA produced an updated coaching manual since 1990? Coaches don't have the support they need. It is the FA's role, mandated by UEFA, to qualify the coaches. It is something we cannot control, but we are discussing it most times when we sit down with the FA.'

In its defence, the FA does seem to recognise its responsibilities to coaches. In 2008, it launched a new coach education strategy called Developing World Class Coaches and Players, a four-year plan to 'address the major issues in coaching and player development which include fundamental questions around what, how, when and where we teach the game'.

The plan presents an honest, if dismal, appraisal of where England stands in terms of coaching, 'Insufficient numbers of high-quality English players, coaches and tutors means that it is time to reverse recent trends and formulate a clear, integrated plan across the professional and national games to effect change and raise standards across the coaching workforce,' reads the report's introduction.

Sir Trevor Brooking notes that 'radical change and investment is needed', while the FA's head of coaching, John Peacock, states that, 'In comparison to our European counterparts, we do not place the same degree of importance on the status of coaching in this country.' He continues, 'This must change if we are going to progress. There has to be a genuine desire to create a coaching culture in which coaching is considered a profession.'

The plan lays out a range of new qualifications and admits England is thousands, and in some categories, tens of thousands of qualified coaches short of the numbers in comparison to other leading European football countries. It also outlines delivery of a new range of age-appropriate courses for academy and centre of excellence staff, including an academy manager's licence, and specialist age coaching courses for 5 to 11 year olds, 12 to 16 year olds, and 17 to 21 year olds.

There are ambitious plans to have 1 million English 5- to 11-year-old children coached in the FA's Tesco Skills programme at grass roots level. But it sets modest aims in terms of the number of elite coaches it plans to develop by 2012. While the plan envisages some 100,000 people will take the basic Level One coaching badge, with 10,000 taking the Level Two qualification, when it gets to more serious levels just 2,500 coaches are predicted to train for UEFA B (Level Four) and just 100 at UEFA A – a senior coaching qualification. Just 40 people will take the Pro Licence (the very top qualification, designed for coaches primarily at Premier League and international level).

The FA see their much vaunted National Football Centre at Burton-upon-Trent as the future 'hub' of their training programmes. However, at the time of writing, Burton looks little closer to completion than it did several years ago when the original building work stopped. Howard Wilkinson, who always saw its development as a key part of an elite coaching plan to accompany the academies, puts up a convincing case for what it could achieve, 'It would have symbolic importance. It is a gesture that we mean business,' said Wilkinson. 'You can look at coach education, you can look at referee education, you can build integration between county FAs, schools, grass roots and the professional game. All the people under one roof, mixing together, meeting, exchanging ideas, there would be a cross-fertilisation of sports science, medicine and technical staff.

'You could arrange meetings and events. Part of its function would be as a college. It can be a place to train, to run mini-tournaments for the grass roots game, a place for players going straight from playing into concentrated coaching courses, designed to deal with the demands of professional football. You could look at the game as a whole.'

Sadly, the PGYDR failed. Capello had long given up on it – allegedly unimpressed by the lack of technical expertise around the table – before it finally fell apart in January 2009, just nine months after its formation. Wilkinson was described as 'trying to run before he could walk'. In some respects he found himself out of step with the people implementing the youth development system he had revamped back in 1997.

Nonetheless, after the group's final meeting, the chairmen of the three major protagonists paid warm tributes to Wilkinson. Lord Triesman, of the FA, said in a press release: 'We have had the benefit of guidance from one of the country's outstanding coaches. His vision for developing elite players and avoiding losing them from the game deserves to be carried forward by excellent coaches in excellent football centres. All young people are entitled to the best opportunity in every walk of life, not least in football and we aim to stand comparison with the very best.'

An upbeat FA statement said that a new group would be formed and that the FA would push ahead with its new strategy and business plan for the development of coach education. 'The chairmen of the FA, Premier League and Football League have agreed to create new coaching criteria for qualifications – jointly designed by their respective organisations and leading educational institutions,' it read. 'Developing a new children and youth coaching manual will also be among the immediate objectives of the new group – which will involve representatives from the FL, PL and the FA. It replaces the previous Professional Game Youth Development Group (PGYDG).'

It is hard to have any confidence that the backbiting will abate, just by changing the name of the committee. Regardless of its name or terms of reference, the new committee is unlikely to involve Howard Wilkinson. A football man through and through, Wilkinson was originally ushered into the FA in 1997 as the voice of professional football. Apart from drafting the *Charter for Quality*, Wilkinson's main achievement during his tenure was in articulating the views of the country's coaches – many of whom are reticent about expressing their opinions too publicly for fear of the damage it might do to their future careers. But the man who had called for 'unity' when drafting the charter found himself – 11 years later – grimly trying to hold things together. When interviewed shortly after the PGYDG had collapsed, he was understandably downbeat. 'Without joined-up thinking the root problems will not be tackled,' he said. In many ways he saw himself as a flag bearer. But at 65, maybe he felt it was time for someone else to come in. 'It needs a new banner waver, but the danger is if you are a banner waver and you are not successful people say "there he goes again. He can't be right because nothing he says ever happens".'

Of course, the bigger question is can football survive as one of the major social and cultural forces in this country despite the fact that no one in the professional game is preparing for the future? Can it survive and be as healthy as it is now if the English national team fails even to qualify for the World Cup or the European Championships? Wilkinson is not so sure, 'I had academy directors and centre of excellence managers who talked to me and said, "keep at it – don't stop talking and making people listen. We need you to keep going – you articulate what we think better than most." But I have said, "yeah, but I'm not getting anywhere, fellas".'

Small wonder that back at the coalface of youth development there is anger and frustration. 'The politics are restricting the new FA coaching strategy,' fumed Dave Parnaby at Middlesbrough. 'It advocates better coaches, better players and better facilities. Who can argue with that?

'The youth development group fell apart. Why? Because of politics and self-interest. We have been promised change – and we are all waiting – but nothing is happening. We have been talking about the same subject for three or four years now.'

'Don't talk me to me about politics,' says Aston Villa's Brian Jones in frustration. 'Until you have one authority running youth development you might as well forget it.' Jones would like to see some of the country's experienced youth developers actually involved in the discussion – but claims they are kept at arms length. 'I look at people like Dave Richardson [chairman of the Professional Football Coaches Association], Liam Brady [Arsenal's academy director] and Jim Cassell [Manchester City academy director] – why don't we use their wealth of experience and knowledge?'

This isn't the first issue on which football's governors have been found wanting. If they cannot agree to act to protect the children they are coaching, registering as players and swapping around for cash – maybe they will need legislation foisted upon them. Is there a role for government in all this? 'Yes there is,' says Andy Burnham, Secretary of State for Culture, Media and Sport, whose office is a short walk from the FA's headquarters in Soho Square. 'The game is better regulated and the culture in the game is changing, but there can never be any room for complacency.'

He is keen to shift the focus away from the politics and back to the interests of the players – the boys and parents committing themselves to football academies – who have been lost in the debate. 'In terms of inspections there is a strong case for independent assessment. There is an unbalanced power relationship between the parents and the club. When it comes to the welfare of the boys and their education you can never be complacent,' he said.

'I would never accept the argument that everything is OK because it can't always be. The drive is always to empower parents and help them make an informed choice and I will push to see this. What is lacking is independent authoritative information so people facing that have their son's welfare in mind. This is not personal criticism, but vested interests arrive very quickly and are making a case from a vested interest point of view,' Burnham concluded.

What is arguably missing from football academies are the sort of independent standards that are laid out in education by law. Indeed, an emphasis on the education of players by clubs and the response of schools, colleges and universities to the professional football clubs' academies has been profound.

CHAPTER 9

EDUCATION, EDUCATION, EDUCATION

At 10.30 on a Monday morning a boy doing indoor school football training receives a vicious whack in the face from a ball inadvertently kicked in his direction. It fells him. Dazed, confused and in tears he is helped from the pitch. Someone calls for the physio. A physiotherapist? At school? On hand to treat kids playing sport? What kind of elite establishment is this?

It's not, actually. The boy is a member of Watford FC's academy – and the indoor pitch is the latest kind of 3G surface – as close to grass as you can get. But this isn't the club's own private facility – it is the Harefield Academy. Sounds posh, but actually this is one of the government's re-branded schools, part of their academies initiative – a fancy-sounding moniker given to former failing schools which have been spruced up and re-opened under a new guise.

The Harefield Academy is an impressive sight. Built at a cost of £24 million in 2005, it replaced what was a failing institution, John Penrose School, on the same site with money from the Private Finance Initiative (PFI) and co-funded by the Department for Education and Skills (DfES), the London Borough of Hillingdon and private investment from three Watford FC directors, David Meller, Mike Sherwood and Haig Oundjian.

Not that this is your average failing inner city school surrounded by urban deprivation. The school is set in the village of Harefield on the north-west edge of the London Borough of Hillingdon, close to the south Hertfordshire green belt and just inside the M25 orbital route. The school will eventually have capacity for some 750 students aged 11 to 15, and a further 250 post-16 students. Its huge open atrium is light, bright and airy – and resembles a modern urban museum more than a school. The cafe serves cappuccinos and lattes, while banks of PCs on which kids can study or just surf the Internet are lined up on open workspaces rather than tucked away in classrooms. It looks great.

The sports facilities are magnificent. There is a gym with weights and machines, not just the worn out pommel horse we had at my secondary school, and the indoor 3G is fantastic. Just as well, because it is hammering down outside and without this I don't know what sort of quality coaching could take place on the day of my visit.

Three-quarters of Watford FC's 12- to 16-year-old academy players are educated here in what is an innovative, integrated approach to balancing the holistic needs of boys training to be elite sportsmen, but staying on track with their education.

The first intake of Watford players started here in September 2008 so it is too early to deduce the outcome, but this has the feel of a project that will work – and is a local solution to local needs. The club isn't prising the players away from their mates and familiar surroundings by tucking them away in a private school. This place meets their football and education needs on one site, with their football training shaped around their regular school day.

The Monday morning session I'm watching is little more than the stretching out of any aches and strains from matches played the day before. The boy caught by the enthusiastically struck volley is treated within seconds by the physio – although, in reality, there isn't a lot he can do other than apply the age old 'magic sponge', tell the boy to sit the session out, dry his tears, clear his head and make him smile at an idiotic visiting journalist who tries to make him forget his woes by saying, 'Phew, I bet *that* hurt!'

The school day starts at 8.15 a.m. for all pupils, with the first football session for the Watford FC boys between 9.30 and 11 a.m. The players eat straight afterwards – allowing them time to digest their food before the afternoon session, which runs from 2.15 to 4.15 p.m. They don't miss any school time.

A full team of academy support staff are here – not just a full-time physiotherapist, but coaches and Watford's education and welfare officer, Ian Smithson. Under their watchful eyes the boys will do a further session in the afternoon after more school lessons. Their educational 'catch up' time for missing conventional afternoon lessons will be late in the afternoon. These are proper lessons taught by teaching staff and not just some kind of general studies free time when they are let loose on the Internet until home time. It is a properly planned education programme.

The players complete their day, sport and education, by 6 p.m. – the very hour when most boys attending football academies and centres of excellence are turning up for training. The lads at the Harefield Academy, meanwhile, have the rest of the evening at home, and turn up refreshed and ready to go the next day. 'There is no competition for their time,' says Tim Ball, Watford's academy business manager, whose 13-year-old son Dominic is among the 50 academy players attending the school. Incidentally, Ball's other son, Matthew, travels to Norwich City's academy from Welwyn Garden City, which is just inside the catchment area – so it is fair to say that the Ball household is fully aware of the disruption this can cause.

At present, most of Watford's players either travel here on the club minibus, by taxi or under their own steam – although an accommodation block is being built at the school to cater for students (not just the Watford footballers).

This is a far cry from the experience of many youngsters and their parents at some of the country's academies and centres of excellence, whose commitments in terms of time alone can be horrific. Hours off at work, rushed journeys, missed homework and disturbed eating patterns are more likely to lead to days off school than to produce fit and energetic young footballers.

But the luxury of time is not the only benefit for the boys at Harefield. 'They mix with all the normal kids – so they meet the fat 'uns, thin 'uns, short 'uns and tall 'uns,' says Ball. It is a win-win-win situation – for the boys, for Watford FC, who can monitor the education of their players and for the school, who have the prestige of playing permanent host to a Championship-level football club academy.

There is no animosity between the school and the football club. No one is pretending there won't be problems, because when all is said and done these are teenage boys. Education and welfare officer Ian Smithson joins us for a chat. Unlike his counterparts at other clubs this is, effectively, where he works most of the time. He doesn't have to flit between schools, trying to patch up damaged relationships caused by the odd word out of line from an errant coach. If he needs to speak to players or teachers about any issues they, and he, are here.

There is symmetry, too. Watford's Under-10s coach Dave Godley was one of the players who developed at Cirencester's innovative college academy. Just as Cirencester Town had looked to a collaboration between a non-League club and an imaginative further education college to develop young footballers back in 1995, so Watford did in 2008. Nick Cox, the Under-16s coach, has progressed from Watford FC's community programme and understands the social value of the work they are doing. 'It isn't our own high tech academy – but it is a good solution to our needs,' said Cox.

It isn't difficult to pick holes in what Harefield and Watford are doing. What happens to kids when they are released from the academy – where do they go for their education? Watford insist they will retain their places at the school – but will the club still pick them up and drop them off from home? Will the boys want to come to an academy where – dragging their broken hearts around the school – they can see the other academy players laughing, joking, smiling, getting on, moving forward in football? Possibly not.

Other concerns might be that the school goes hell for leather to enter school football competitions, urging the Watford academy players to represent them – an unfair advantage possibly over other 'normal' schools in the area, and totally understandable as Harefield attempts to gain a sporting reputation for its academy, if only as a means of attracting future talented students. Other critics say 'yes, but how many sports academies are there? It isn't an option for most clubs.' These are all valid criticisms, but Watford are not claiming they have developed a panacea for all ills; this just suits their needs.

It's obviously a scheme well worth checking out. 'Bet you're run off your feet showing other clubs around, aren't you?' I asked Tim Ball.

Amazingly, he answered, 'A handful of clubs have been here.' You might have expected clubs, particularly those at the peeling paint-end of the Football League, to investigate this sort of scheme and work out how they might adapt it to suit the needs of their own youth players. Apparently not.

After an initial blaze of publicity, which attracted interest from Spanish club Valencia, the Spanish FA, the English Premier League, Charlton Athletic, Darlington and Newcastle United, Sir Trevor Brooking from the FA, together with Dave Parnaby and John McDermott, academy managers at Middlesbrough and Spurs respectively, there hasn't been much interest from anyone else.

Time will tell if the Watford FC and Harefield Academy association proves successful – or maybe we will never know. 'Would we have produced these players anyway?' muses Ball. 'The proof will be if we produce lots of first-team players and some go on to do well educationally. Either way, we will be happy.'

The need to get a good education is exemplified by the story of a former player signed to Watford's academy who grew up in Harrow, just a few miles from Harefield, and moved to Luton at the age of 12. Like so many boys, Ricky Clarke thought he had the football world at his feet. When I interviewed him at the age of 22, Clarke recalled signing a four-year contact for Watford ten years earlier. 'I was paraded on the pitch with three other players as the future of Watford FC – signing our contracts on the pitch and shaking hands with Elton John. I thought this is it – this is what my life is going to be – I am going to be a professional footballer. No doubt about it.'

Ricky had already been on Watford's books for three years. 'I signed my first one-year contract when I was nine years old,' he recalls, having been spotted aged seven playing for a local club in Harrow. 'A few clubs came in for me including Chelsea – the team I supported,' remembers Clarke, who instead of deciding to go on trial at his favourite club, made the kind of heart-glowing pact that young boys do. With a couple of mates from his junior club they all opted to go to Watford together – all for one, one for all.

'I was training three times a week, on Tuesday and Thursday evenings, on Saturday mornings, and playing matches on Sunday, from the age of 9 to 12.' After moving to secondary school, Ricky was required to ditch school sport – even though he had enjoyed playing both football and rugby: he was the future of Watford after all. Occasionally he would break the embargo, as much to play with his schoolmates as anything else. Ricky doesn't defend these decisions – and isn't bitter towards anything that happened to him – they were just the healthy excesses of youth. 'My life was football, football, football whereas my mates were going on skiing holidays and out on quad bikes,' said Ricky. 'They were having fun and I felt I was missing out.'

Dave Woollaston, who has been quoted throughout this book, is an English Schools FA coach and a careers teacher at Icknield High School in Luton, which Ricky attended. He recalls a helpful, willing pupil – even playing in goal in one school game in an attempt to avoid injury and prevent Watford finding out. 'He just wanted to participate and help out his mates, bless him,' said Woollaston.

'I didn't really do much school work to be honest because after I had signed the 4-year contract at 12 I didn't think I needed to bother,' said Ricky. 'I thought my world would be a professional footballer's life, but it didn't work out and now I wish I had done a lot more school work.

'I don't think I would have had time to do any homework anyway. I wasn't the brightest kid. I didn't particularly like learning or being in the classroom because I had football and I didn't think I needed to learn.'

But a triple whammy was heading his way – injury, pressure and disenchantment with playing the game. 'At 15, I got a really bad back injury so Watford released me. I felt myself slipping down the ladder and my performance went downhill. I think they just look after you that bit more if you are a shining player – and I was that player from 9 to 14, and then it slipped away. I felt under pressure at 14 and 15 because my mum had put so much time and effort in getting me to where I needed to go … you start to fall out of love with football because you are doing it so much. It becomes a routine because you have been doing it from such a young age. When I was younger I couldn't get enough of it.'

Ricky left school with three GCSEs and joined Rushden and Diamonds, at the time a Football League club, on a two-year scholarship, where he briefly rediscovered his appetite for the game. At Rushden, Ricky says he was 'loving it and buzzing,' but had a groin strain that kept him sidelined for three months. 'The club looked after me but you miss out and it is hard to get back in.' At 18 years old, he was released and although he played semi-professionally at Dunstable Town, he then drifted into local football.

When I spoke to him Ricky had plans to get back into the game – but he still feels he made an enormous sacrifice. 'It was a mistake to choose football over other things. Looking back, I should have carried on with my education and just tried a lot harder at school and seen how my football went.' The sort of co-ordinated approach at Watford FC and Harefield Academy would definitely have helped a player like Ricky Clarke.

'Education, education, education' was how Tony Blair set out his priorities for government at the Labour Party Conference of September 1996 – fairly sure in the knowledge that he would soon be bounding through the doors of 10 Downing Street, which happened with a thumping landslide the following spring. At the same time Howard Wilkinson was putting the finishing touches to *A Charter for Quality* which, although it also put the interests of the child first and called for the mandatory introduction of education and welfare officers at football club academies and centres of excellence, was simply too thin on detail.

OK, it encouraged clubs to work with schools – but in many instances this was done in a crass, cack-handed manner. PE teachers weren't necessarily in the mood to co-operate. They were being robbed of their best footballers, who were being told that signing for an academy meant they could no longer play for the school team and, in some cases, were even being dissuaded by clubs from participating in other school sports or other activities they deemed dangerous. They were interfering with the education and social upbringing of boys – and giving nothing back.

Like many teachers, Dave Woollaston has often been placed in an awkward position – sometimes having to decide whether to allow boys who have played in academies, but are suddenly released, back into school representative teams at the expense of boys who haven't. 'I have to be loyal to the boys who are loyal to me,' insisted Woollaston.

Other teachers were spotting hopelessly tired boys crawling into school in the morning, knackered, because of their commitments to football academies. This was a whole new ball game. It was not the integrated approach shaped at the FA National School for a select group of talented 14 to 16 year olds. It was ad hoc policy shaped by an industry that views the boys as commodities – a belief expressed among the FA's upper echelons at Soho Square, at the English Schools' FA, and a major point of concern for the Secretary of State for Culture, Media and Sport, Andy Burnham.

It wouldn't have been this way if football clubs had proceeded with caution. There is little doubt that most people – the clubs, the players, schools and parents – would prefer their children to receive their football education closer to school time to help the boys strive towards the 10,000 hours it takes to train a talented athlete from 'Pitch to Podium'. Clubs enviously cast their eyes to Europe and blame the lack of time they have with boys in comparison.

But it isn't eggs for eggs. Sport doesn't have to be a major part of the schools curriculum in countries like Holland, where the school day finishes earlier than in the UK, because local sports clubs are integrated in the community – they can take on that extra duty, because they work with all children. English clubs want to hive off only the best for their own interest in their own academies, tucked away from the community in the quiet countryside.

With children playing in football academies and falling behind with their education, the danger is that they get left behind for life. For a careers teacher like Dave Woollaston, who has to advise pupils who wish to take all sorts of career paths, football presents a distinct problem. 'From a careers perspective, if you have a pupil who wants to be a doctor and they fail there are still plenty of other jobs they go into and lots of other options, but the boy who gives everything to football has nowhere to go.

'When they hear the words "sorry, but we don't think you're good enough," they don't want to play football anymore – and in the classroom suddenly you are teaching traumatised youngsters for maybe six months afterwards. Most of their time is spent looking for other clubs to join while rushing towards them are their GCSEs, so they aren't fully focussed on them.'

Times are changing though. In recent years, after a faltering start, the academies have started to bring professionalism to the delivery of education. The old days of youth players being used as cheap ground staff have been consigned to history. Since 1983 they have been replaced by Youth Trainee Schemes (YTS). Although the schemes offered a wide range of vocational and academic options (trainees studied on a part-time basis around their training) they often lacked support from their clubs. Many players simply took basic courses in leisure management or general studies – meaningless qualifications that offered them very little in terms of a post-playing career. With five out of six players who signed on aged 16 leaving the game before the age of 21, it is a significant problem.

In 2001, I spent a day at a college in the north-west of England attended by scholars from several local Premier and Football League clubs. Most of the players were 17 or 18 years old and in the final few months of their scholarships. They spend the entire day slouched across the tables and chairs chatting about football to a succession of lecturers who seemed to view the lessons as a chance to find out what was happening at their local clubs. This was more about filling time than education. Meaningless doesn't even begin to describe it. When I spoke to some of the players they told me that quite often they didn't even receive this flimsy bit of education. If the clubs decided they wanted them in for extra training, they had first call.

At the other extreme, over at Crewe, Dario Gradi remembers allowing future England striker Dean Ashton, at the time a player obviously destined to make it with dozens of first-team matches under his belt, time off to study for his A levels. 'Just in case,' said Gradi. One tackle, as we know, can end the most promising career. Having education to fall back on isn't an option – it is a necessity.

The situation reached crisis point in 2003 when the Department for Education threatened to withdraw funding for football club schemes. That made the clubs sit up and take notice. 'Funding agencies were concerned that retention and academic achievement were not good enough,' said Alan Sykes, chief executive of a new not-for-profit body that has been formed to deliver education programmes at Football League clubs called League Football Education (LFE). 'When I worked for a football club I'm not sure I really saw the players' education as my problem,' admitted Sykes, a former club secretary at Huddersfield Town and chief executive at Sheffield Wednesday.

'A young player might be learning to do a practical trade, such as bricklaying for example, and he would go on day release to college for one-and-a-half days a week. But he would then go back to the club to continue his training as a footballer. The other boys at college went back to building sites to work on the skills they'd learned – so the following week the football trainee hadn't had the same opportunity to work on the skills he had learned at college and would often fall behind.'

Consequently attainment rates were low – 40 per cent of scholars didn't complete their courses, and among those who did less than 35 per cent actually passed their course.

'What we have said to Football League clubs is, "look, if you want to continue to receive money from the funding agencies you are going to have to treat the matter with respect and support the apprentices through the education programme or the funding will be withdrawn." We have got a massive buy-in to that ethos with clubs now producing very high standards and running excellent programmes,' said Sykes.

There was a similar situation in the Premier League. 'When we offered players lots of different career options they sometimes fell between two stools – not quite meeting their educational needs or the demands on them as footballers', explained Mike Foster. 'Too often a boy could go through a two-year elite development programme at a professional club, but wouldn't be taken on by the club and would walk away with nothing to show for it.'

The result has been the Apprenticeship in Sporting Excellence (ASE), a scheme used by many sports, which was introduced into professional football in the summer of 2004. The scheme is co-funded by the Learning and Skills Council and the PFA. 'This was a specific educational programme for elite athletes designed by SkillsActive in consultation with football clubs. LFE was formed to deliver ASE for all Football League clubs,' said Sykes.

Whether players are working towards a Premier League football scholarship or a Football League apprenticeship, they are aiming for the same goal on the ASE programme. Their Football Development Programme (FDP) will incorporate pre-season training and preparation, coaching, tactics, fitness training, mental skills development, participation in matches, assessment and feedback. Completion of the FDP leads to the award of a National Vocational Qualification (NVQ) in Sporting Excellence – a Level 3 qualification, nationally recognised as the equivalent of an A level.

The education programme involves 780 hours of guided learning during the two years of the scholarship or apprenticeship, and consists of a technical certificate, key skills and other short courses. The technical certificate provides boys with the theory behind the practice – with scholars or apprentices usually going to a local college for a day-and-a-half a week to study relevant subjects such as nutrition, fitness, psychology and physiology, all of which are important to elite athletes.

This usually leads to a BTEC qualification in sporting performance and excellence and is awarded at either Level 2 (equivalent to four higher grade GCSEs) or Level 3 (equivalent to two A levels). The level taken by the scholar or apprentice normally depends on his previous achievements at school.

In special cases, traditional A level courses may be taken. Other short courses include instruction in the laws of the game, which is compulsory, FA coaching courses and diversity training. A club is not compelled to take part in the ASE programme, but if it chooses to run a separate programme it must be accredited by either the Premier League or the Football League.

On the face of it, the ASE programme has been one of the success stories to emerge from the academy and centres of excellence system. 'In 2008 our retention rate was 91 per cent,' said Sykes, 'You'll always have some drop out, as some young players find the transition into full-time football too physically demanding, while some just realise that it's not for them. This figure will be hard to beat, but we are delighted with the tremendous progress with retention on the programme.'

I wondered whether the results were more remarkable because, rather like Ricky Clarke, many of the boys who had been in academies or centres of excellence had slipped behind with their education, convinced they were going to make it as professional footballers and therefore thought they had no need to do school work? 'Each year we encounter a number of boys who have switched off mainstream education, because they have been so convinced they were going to make it as a professional footballer that for the previous two or three years they haven't put the effort in that is needed,' said Sykes.

'When apprentices start the programme we give them a diagnostic test. Time and time again we see boys who have come out of school with no qualifications at all, but when we put them through the test they actually turn out to be quite a bit better then their exam results suggest.

'We wouldn't be producing figures of 88 per cent if apprentices were very poor academically. They must have latent ability – it is just a question of bringing it out. The holistic support the players receive today is light years away from what it used to be. I'm proud to say LFE's contribution has been substantial in working with clubs and showing them how important it is to provide the right level of support to apprentices.

'The last four years have seen tremendous progress in the development of the apprenticeship programme. Clubs are very supportive of ASE and young apprentices are now receiving extremely high levels of care, attention, academic support and technical development, all designed to produce better footballers for the future.'

The Premier League education programmes are fronted by another new body, Premier League Learning. Education inspectors seem happy with the football education programmes, 'The fact we had a good Ofsted report seems to suggest we have reached a good standard,' said Mike Foster. 'It means an independent body thinks we are doing a good job. We have also recently been awarded the Training Quality Standard for the delivery of our scholarship programme.

'In 2007-08, 78 per cent boys got either the NVQ or BTEC qualification compared with the national average of 64 per cent,' added Foster. 'Between 2005-06 and 2007-08, the number of boys achieving full framework who progressed from a scholarship to a professional contract increased from 45 to 60 per cent.

'Now, at least, players can walk away with a certificate that is the equivalent of two A levels. I don't know what currency that has in the educational world, but it is better than where we were.'

Opinion remains divided.

Aston Villa's education and welfare officer, Paul Brackwell, who confessed he used to feel like the 'lone ranger' for standing up for the value of player education, has altered his opinion about the breadth of courses on offer. 'I used to think a wide range of courses, vocations and subjects available to study was a good thing. But I've changed my mind. I now believe that if a player has selected football as his chosen path that is the area he should study.'

Other educationalists disagree. 'The introduction of the ASE Programme within professional football is more about providing a costing shortcut rather than providing good academic pathways for young individuals,' says Jamie Bennett, a former trainee at Mansfield Town, who went on a sports scholarship to the United States to successfully study for a sports management degree and now runs a company called Sports Ed, which organises trips for students seeking to take the same path. 'Everyone ends up doing the same meaningless course. There isn't enough variation to allow players to do the courses they want – only courses that fit around football. It is easy to pass, so it looks like the courses are achieving wonderful pass rates. The problem is that if you want to progress to higher education these qualifications are just not good enough.'

Glyn Harding, a senior lecturer in sports coaching at University of Worcester, who was an education and welfare officer at Wolverhampton Wanderers and a former schoolteacher, agrees. 'The ASE programme doesn't sit right with me. The high achievers are treading water. Some guys are pushed through and there is a group in the middle for whom it is a tick-box exercise. How much real learning is going on? Is it about passing a course or achieving something? I am not sure.'

Harding has several students who play semi-professional football and has seen some of his past students go into the professional game after completing their degrees. He has also worked with a number of former professional players, but says none of them were chosen because they had taken the ASE programme. 'They came here with a mixture of qualifications and abilities,' said Harding. 'But they specialise – some do outdoor pursuits, some do sports studies, some do sports science, some do coaching, and some teach. You can break the teaching down to early years, primary, secondary and post graduate. So there are lots of options. You cannot say one package fits everybody and that is the problem with ASE.'

Aside from universities offering sports scholarships, the burgeoning college football academies, which picked up on Cirencester College's lead and offer a greater degree of academic flexibility, mean that thousands of boys are graduating from college with more meaningful qualifications than their professional club counterparts studying the ASE programme. 'We frequently have students who attend our football academy who go on to higher education,' said Nigel Robbins at Cirencester College, who admits it is harder now to pick up talented footballers than when they started in 1995: 'We don't get the same quality of players anymore because there are so many other colleges offering football programmes, but academically I am delighted by our achievements,' said Robbins.

'I fear for those boys in professional club academies because they might have found employment fairly easy to come by if they weren't taken on by their clubs at 18 or 19, because the job market has been quite good, but while the credit crunch continues I am not sure the same opportunities will be available to them.'

However, Jamie Bennett, who was a soccer coach at West Nottinghamshire College in Mansfield, also dismisses the many UK college football scholarships as a 'number-crunching exercise' devised by college management to secure funding for individuals at the college. 'Football is a great carrot to achieve this,' said Bennett. 'It only produces a small percentage of professional players into the game and doesn't always work because the [semi-professional] clubs don't have the money or expertise to support it.'

There is, of course, another educational responsibility football clubs have to their young players, whether at academy and centre of excellence level, or as senior professionals, to teach them personal discipline and financial management. It would be easy to cite any number of examples where players have been poor role models and become entangled in incidents in nightclubs, pubs and restaurants, sometimes resulting in prison sentences.

A cautionary tale comes from a player who, in the pre-academy days, thought he had the world at his feet. Jason Blunt was an England Under-18 international who played in midfield behind Michael Owen and Emile Heskey and in front of Jamie Carragher – all players who went on to become senior internationals. Blunt made his Premier League debut for Leeds United alongside defender Ian Harte, and was in the same youth team as Harry Kewell.

By the age of 21 he was out of English professional football and declared bankrupt.

Jason blames no one but himself for this. He had underachieved at school, just another player who, mistakenly, thought he didn't need to bother because he was destined to be a footballer. Born in Penzance, Cornwall, Jason had been adopted and raised in Barnsley. He was courted by several clubs including Manchester United, Sheffield Wednesday and Everton, before eventually signing for Leeds United at the age of 14.

At Leeds, he did a two-year YTS, although his education stayed firmly on the back burner. Jason recalls doing one half-day release to attend college to study leisure and tourism on Monday afternoons – and he didn't always attend the lectures.

'Looking back,' says Blunt, 'I had little guidance for the life I was going into.' He recalls being taken to a bank by Paul Hart, at the time youth development manager at Leeds, who showed him how to withdraw money from a cash machine. Jason got the hang of it pretty well in the following years.

His football development was exceptional. He made his Premier League debut aged 18, in March 1996 against Middlesbrough, whose team included Juninho and Fabrizio Ravanelli, among the first wave of genuine international stars flooding into English football. First Division champions in 1991-92, Leeds were managed at the time by Howard Wilkinson and their ranks included the likes of Tomas Brolin, Gary Speed, Gary McAllister and Carlton Palmer.

After the Middlesbrough game, Jason did well enough to earn subsequent starts against Southampton and Nottingham Forest, but Wilkinson was under pressure as Leeds struggled for results. He rested Blunt and another young midfielder, Lee Bowyer. Despite this setback, a bright future appeared to be on the cards, yet those three games proved to be the peak of Jason's career.

Suddenly earning £1,000 a week aged just 18, he started spending his wages on drink and cars. Following Wilkinson's dismissal, Blunt fell out of favour with his successor, George Graham, and after an unsuccessful loan spell at Raith Rovers, he joined former Leeds defender Nigel Worthington, in his first managerial role, at Blackpool in the 1997-98 season. 'It was brilliant at first,' recalled Jason. Yet after a few games he was dropped and was eventually released, nine months into a two-year contract. He slid deep into debt and, unable to pay his bills and with a baby girl to support, was declared bankrupt. 'It was a huge relief to have the debts lifted off my back,' recalls Blunt.

Who knows what might have happened next? Fortunately, he was advised to move to Italy, where he played firstly for Castellaneta and later, Grottaglie, both based in the Puglia region of southern Italy. He led a cleaner, healthier life – paying more attention to diet and nutrition (a coach once scrunched up a bread roll that Jason had opted for during a meal, to show him how it would sit in his stomach).

Understandably missing his family, Jason returned to England at the age of 23 and played for a succession of non-League clubs – Scarborough, Doncaster Rovers (with whom he won the Conference play-off final), Tamworth and Alfreton Town, while studying for a qualification in sports science.

In 2005, he got a lucky break and took a job teaching PE at a private school in Wakefield. He does some part-time coaching now, but isn't involved in professional football anymore. 'I had some good and bad luck,' said Blunt, looking back. 'But it was no one else's fault but my own.'

Some lessons are learned the hard way.

CHAPTER 10

MANY A TEAR HAS TO FALL

'Many a tear has to fall ... but it's all in the game'
American singer Tommy Edwards in *'It's All in the Game'*

For the lucky 1 per cent of players who make it through the youth development system from the age of nine, their life as a professional footballer can be an amazing experience. But the sad fact is that the overwhelming majority of players being spotted and signed by clubs from ever younger ages are pushed out of the game along the way.

According to those who have to dole out the bad news, the hardest job in football is telling young players they are going to be released. You just cannot sugar the pill. 'There is no easy way to say it, so there is no point going around the houses, you just have to look them in the eye and tell them the truth,' said much-travelled football manager and former Scottish international, Bruce Rioch. 'The tears often fall. It hurts the young boys. You are shattering the dreams they have worked at for years. I always say, "It is only my opinion. It isn't fact. Go away and prove me wrong and no one will be more delighted than me." Then you thank them for their time and effort and always shake their hand.'

Some clubs are known to have their chaplain on hand – a move akin to a priest accompanying wartime officials who had to tell a mother that their son has died in battle. It has always been a tough call – but one that has to be made. The decent thing is that it is done with care and compassion.

No facet of youth development needs to be handled with greater sensitivity by academies and centres of excellence – especially now that professional clubs are recruiting boys at pre-teen ages and use development centres as a means of burrowing down to children who are little more than toddlers in the elusive search for young talent.

What you don't do is use harsh words, like the man who told six-year-old Jack that he had been 'culled'. 'Exit strategies', as the football industry calls them, need to be shaped and carried out as planned. Some clubs put a lot of time and thought into these plans, such as how and where boys and their parents would best hear the sad news. 'It is the end of the dream,' muses Dave Parnaby at Middlesbrough. 'The emotions are no different if they are 9 or 19 years old. We have tried to learn from our experiences. What we say to parents when they join is this, "if it comes to a point where your boy has to leave us how would you like us to let you know?"

'We advise the parents that in our opinion their son is better off hearing the disappointing decision in his home environment with his mum and dad. But we always ask them whether they'd like a phone call or a letter, or whether they'd like to come in to the academy, by themselves or with the boy as well.

'The one thing we don't want is a very emotional boy with a lot of adrenalin, getting upset. It's not easy for anyone. But that scenario is very rare. What we are finding more and more is that parents and players are receiving the news and saying "thanks for the experience, thanks for the time," and asking, "what would you advise him to do next?" It's not easy for us either, because we get attached to the players. But we make sure they know that they are always welcome and it is a pleasure to see or hear from them.'

There is also debate about the best time of year to tell the players. Brian Jones at Aston Villa is in favour of letting them know as soon as possible so that they can find another club. 'This is something that needs to be examined much more closely,' says Jones. 'We make decisions before Christmas so that they have two or three months to come to terms with the fact we won't be offering them a contract.

'But we also say, "Please don't think that when you drive out through the gate that is the end of your contact with Aston Villa.

Please continue to come in and receive your coaching right up to the end of the season if necessary because you need to keep fit and develop your skills so that if another club offers you training then you are ready to take them up and make the most of it."'

However, Alan Sykes at League Football Education (LFE) believes that, for older boys in particular, that approach is fraught with danger. 'If you tell them too early it will affect your retention. Our best practice guide is not to tell them before April as some boys will walk out and will regret it later, but they may miss the assessment trials and careers days, which may help them in future. Clubs will also have the opportunity to play them in a few games, to put them in the shop window if you like. We have a dedicated team in LFE who work on exit and progression, providing career exhibitions and exit trials, and we are now working hard to develop partnerships with potential employers and universities.'

Graham Hawkins, head of player development at the Football League, says the news shouldn't come as a surprise to either the player or his parents if the process and report stages have been handled properly, 'You do hear of unhappy parents. We always say to clubs, "If that boy or parent is surprised, then your reporting has been poor." They should not be surprised and should always be kept informed and updated on what is going on.'

The very least you would expect football clubs to want is to have players and parents leave them on such good terms that they will think kindly of the club and will be fans for life. It doesn't take a commercial manager or financial whizz-kid to see the potential value of having a veritable stream of young boys hooked on their local club. Sadly, this is football we're talking about – English football to be precise – and while there are bound to be examples of bad news being handled well by some clubs and coaches, there have also been some appalling instances.

One such story was related to me by a sports teacher who had a 12-year-old pupil at his school who was with a prominent professional club academy and knew he was likely to be released in the near future. The teacher had a good relationship with a number of professional clubs at the time – he had 20 boys at various academies and centres of excellence – and went out of his way to make sure their best interests were being served. Knowing that this particular boy's club had a penchant for informing players they were being released by letter, he pleaded with them to make sure it didn't arrive at the boy's house on his forthcoming 13th birthday. Of course, it did, among his birthday cards. How careless. How heartbreaking. Small wonder that this supportive teacher describes the football business as 'cut-throat'.

I have been told of a boy who was released a few days after his dad had been carjacked with the boy in the car at the time. His dad had been hurled out of the car, kicked senseless and had his wallet stolen. The lad was shocked and traumatised – who wouldn't be? But he was determined to carry on with his football (to many boys, in such circumstances, this is an obvious reaction) so he decided to return to training just two weeks after the incident. He was instantly released. They had found another goalkeeper in his age range and muttered something about lack of commitment. You know where he was going when the carjacking happened, don't you?

In Chapter 5 we first met Jamie – attending a Football League academy where 13-year-old players were being put through their paces until they were physically sick – and his dad Simon. At 15, after six years with the club, and near the end of the season, a decision was due to be made on Jamie's future. 'I knew the end of season assessment was due,' recalls Simon. 'But when I spoke to one of the other parents I discovered that they had already had their letters confirming their appointments and we hadn't. I phoned the head coach to find out where Jamie stood. After some time I was told that Jamie "might be better off playing at a lower level".

'I didn't really know what to say so I thanked him for the time the club had spent working with him and said, "So, what happens next?" The reaction down the phone was kind of "yeah, whatever". The guy just listened basically until I stopped talking. We heard nothing more from the club. All he has to show for his time there are two team photos which we took – one when they played against Manchester United, the team Jamie supports.' Despite being asked to join a non-League club, Jamie declined.

Interviewed again recently, Simon said, 'He has taken a year off from football. He might start again next season, but personally I doubt it. I don't think he will play football again at all. He was a good player too, even if I do say so myself. He seems happy playing golf and going to the gym.'

It is sad and quite shocking to hear that boys feel so depressed by their experience that they want to give up playing completely. Disappointment is one thing – being so hurt by the process that they no longer want to play football ever again is another. There has to be something fundamentally wrong with the way some boys are released.

Nathan Wall didn't even have any photos of the four years he had spent playing at Walsall's centre of excellence. Dad Steven sensed the end was coming – but not the manner in which it came. Like all clubs, Walsall's players receive their assessment reports twice a year and are informed if they will be staying at the club's centre of excellence or not. 'We had been through a few evenings, hadn't we,' said Nathan to his dad, sporting a 'phew, that was close', look on his face. 'I felt nervous before each one.'

Steven had a good idea as to which way the wind was blowing. 'As a parent, looking on, you just get a feeling. I think it had stopped being fun for Nathan, but neither of us wanted to pull the plug. At the end of the day, it is just someone's opinion and I was quite happy with that – the thing I was unhappy about is the way he was released.'

At the interview, Nathan, who was 13 years old at the time, was told he wouldn't be staying, but Steven asked if the club would honour its commitment and continue to coach him because they had signed a two-year contract the previous season. A local council project manager, Steve assumed the deal worked both ways. Not so. 'We were told it was an ongoing contract and if I didn't sign the release form, then they would hold his registration so he couldn't play for any football team at all. I was angry.'

Steven had signed a standard Football League development programme registration form – a YD4 – and he refused to sign Nathan's release form during the meeting, deciding instead to take the matter up with the Football League.

In the meantime Nathan was so upset he couldn't bring himself to say goodbye to the team-mates he'd known over the past four years and he shuffled out of a side door. 'I just couldn't face them,' recalled Nathan. Instead Steven said his goodbyes to the other parents and went to console his son. And that was it. Their 'exit strategy' consisted of little more than one word – 'goodbye'.

When he checked with the Football League, Steven discovered that Walsall had been perfectly entitled to release Nathan without any contractual duty to continue coaching for the rest of the registration period. In essence it means you are tied to the club, but they are not tied to you. They had acted perfectly within their rights. So Steven had to go back to the club with his tail between his legs to sign the release form in order for Nathan to be able to play football elsewhere. 'That was it,' said Steven. 'After four years they offered no help or advice and we had nothing to show for it, bar the signing-on forms. Looking back, Nathan never had any trophies or rewards. 'Kids love mementos, don't they? You'd have thought they would have given them something.'

In common with most clubs, Walsall refused to comment on the issue or discuss individual players, but Glyn Harding, a senior lecturer in sport at University of Worcester, put together a selection of the things they used to present to players and parents when he worked at Wolverhampton Wanderers' academy. It included videos of trips abroad, in particular a tournament in Japan in 2002 just ahead of the World Cup, photo albums featuring images taken on days out to watch international matches, and various booklets. Different strokes for different folks.

Glyn warmly encouraged parents to travel on the coach with their sons to away games – and noted how they would put video packages together of the team playing with a Goal of the Month competition, so the boys could write down why they thought different goals should win and they could win prizes. 'It was a subtle tactic to get them thinking about positive elements of the game,' said Harding.

As a former schoolteacher he understood the value of rewards. 'They are,' he said, 'the little things that make a difference. They make the boys feel special and welcome.' He recalled bumping into one of the players they had to release a few years later. As they chatted, Glyn asked, 'Do you ever watch that video we recorded?'

'Only every night,' was the reply.

'We shouldn't forget these are some of the most memorable times of their lives,' said Harding. 'We should respect them as such.'

For Ryan Craig the end also came swiftly at Coventry City. Father and son were summoned to the club at short notice. 'I was out shopping and received a phone call,' remembers his dad Adrian. 'They said, "Can you come down straight away?". I thought it was important, but wasn't quite sure what it was. They had me and Ryan in the office and said, "Sorry, we're getting rid of him".'

Ryan recalls crying in the car on the way home, 'I just felt really sad because I was losing all my mates.' For Adrian, on one hand it was relief, but on the other anger. 'That was that. They're great when they want you, they're all over you, but as soon they get rid of you, that's it. Goodbye. They just don't care.

'It's every boy's dream to get spotted and signed and to play in top club academy. But when you get there and find it's not what it cracked up to be, it's disappointing,' said Adrian. Still, at least he was relieved of bunking off work early so he could take his 11-year-old son over to the academy for 6 p.m. three times a week.

I interviewed Ryan on BBC Radio Five in May 2007 on a programme about welfare in academies. His voice was a chilling reminder of the harm football's dream factories can do. He was 12 by then and sounded so young and so hurt – so palpably upset. Senior BBC executives at a pre-transmission meeting, who are used to listening to hardened news content, sat up and took notice. 'What happened next?' asked one of them. 'That's it. He's playing local junior football.' There was amazement around the table that a professional club could just let a player go and not offer him anything else.

At the time of that report, Ryan was getting back into playing local junior football again. Adrian had asked Coventry to call the recruitment officer at another West Midlands club, someone well-known among the region's youth football circles who may have been aware of other clubs looking for players, but when Adrian bumped into him at a match a couple of weeks later, the call hadn't been made. Ryan had been left high and dry.

In the end Adrian did his own research and found a club where they play primarily for fun. Does he have any intention of rejoining an academy? 'Maybe later,' he replied. 'When he is older.' At that time you could have taken that as a firm 'no'.

When asked to comment about the Craig's experiences, Coventry didn't feel compelled to provide a specific response. 'Releasing players is the hardest and most upsetting part of our job in the academy,' read a statement they released. 'We have a policy of making these decisions face-to-face, and not via a letter or telephone call.'

They trotted out a familiar line about the vast majority of the players enjoying the experience of playing in their academy – strange really, as the Craigs insist they were not contacted by Coventry City after Ryan's release to see how they had felt about it.

In fact, among the dozens of parents I have spoken to whose children have been with a professional football academy, I don't know of any who have filled in forms requesting feedback or any sort of post-experience questionnaire. 'Not being good enough to be a professional footballer should not be seen as failure,' said Howard Wilkinson. 'We need to work on our after sales service.'

After sales service? It's a bit like being thought of as a car, isn't it? But motor manufacturers are efficient at gathering customer feedback – it is essential to their future business. At the end of the day they are only flogging bits of metal, plastic and rubber. Football clubs deal in flesh and blood and hearts and minds – yet the game's own research on what happens to its junior and youth players after they are released is painfully thin.

So how much research has been done in this area? 'Very little,' admitted Mike Foster of the Premier League. 'Not enough. We have recently commissioned some academic research going back over six years to identify what has become of boys following the completion of their scholarships. We haven't done well enough in the past. We hold our hands up. It is a situation we are addressing.'

In his 2007 review, Richard Lewis mentioned the difficulty of keeping track of players when they are released. But Dr Andy Pitchford at the University of Gloucestershire, co-author of a 2006 report entitled *Child Welfare in Football*, told me that there was a 'culture of secrecy' within the game which makes academies a tough nut to crack for researchers who are trying to build a thorough and authoritative picture of how players and parents view their time attending academies and centres of excellence.

Obviously child protection is a huge issue – and one that must be welcomed within football, as every other area of sport. Surely clubs – capable of operating sophisticated marketing systems when it comes to prising money out of fans' wallets – would welcome independent research into how their business is performing in terms of youth development. But the fact is that the clubs have hobbled along for ten years or more without engaging in and supporting qualitative research among players and parents, which could surely only help and not hinder the process of producing young players, with the result of improved service from the clubs.

One area the game *has* taken seriously in recent years is arranging assessment trials for 16- to 19-year-old players, who play a series of matches over two or three days during February half-term in front of an invited group of club scouts on the lookout for talent. This is an excellent way to help players hook up with new clubs and is organised by the respective leagues.

The Premier League led the way, holding their trials at Lilleshall, however, the Football League has made up ground in recent years, staging what it calls exit and assessment trials at three venues around the country – Bisham Abbey, Lilleshall and Leeds. At present, the trials are only for full-time Premier League scholars and Football League apprentices. Richard Lewis suggested they could be rolled down the age range to enable other players to take advantage of what is obviously a good system.

Of course, the system does have its drawbacks. Many of the boys playing in these matches have only recently discovered that they are being released and are struggling to come to terms with the news. 'It's hard when someone says you're not good enough,' said one of them. Some cynics have likened this parade of players to a meat market – one journalist was even brazen enough to phone the Premier League and ask when the meat market was being held.

But others, like sports psychologist Darren Robinson, who was hired by the Premier League at one of the trials to assist the players, says they face a 'pressure or pleasure' conundrum. 'They are down, but they need to see this as an opportunity to find their feet at a lower level.' Opportunity knocks. The trials work – boys do find new clubs.

Another idea, dreamed up by League Football Education in March 2008, was to stage a careers exhibition at the City of Manchester Stadium, which attracted employers such as Carphone Warehouse, Marks & Spencer and Selfridges as well as several universities. Again, a great idea, but why is there so little of this really great practice?

Meanwhile, over at Aston Villa Brian Jones looks at the problem from another angle. He has a simple solution to reducing the amount of heartache in elite youth development – halve the numbers of boys playing in academies. 'Academies should be for elite players only,' he explained. 'Every boy who comes here should have an opportunity to play professional football. Our academy has the smallest number of schoolboys in the country and we've had that for the past eight years because we will not sign players just to furnish a team.'

Jones believes the rigid game programme rules, which demand full teams at each age group is the main problem. 'If I have a new under-9s squad coming in and we need 13 or 14 players to run it but we can only find nine players that I think are good enough, that is what we'll have.'

Jones merged Villa's under-14 and 15 age groups a few years back – and risked a battle with the Premier League. 'We wanted to be more elitist. Instead of having 32 players registered I had 16 – 8 in each age group – because we wanted better quality. We knew that when it came to offering contracts, 60 to 70 per cent of those players weren't going to be kept on because they weren't good enough.'

Jones wanted to take it further, to other younger age groups. 'You reduce your costs and there is less disappointment among players and parents.' It makes sense. Imagine if the overall number of boys in academies and centres of excellence – currently 10,000 – was halved; that would be 5,000 boys who hadn't unrealistically 'lived the dream'.

FA development director Sir Trevor Brooking agrees, 'There aren't enough good young players who are elite standard. Some clubs will tell you they don't need the numbers of players that they have – and that is where the players and parents get let down.'

Of course, it's not so straightforward, as too many clubs fear miss-ing the valuable players. To them it is more about money than player judgement. For people like Huw Jennings, former head of youth development at the Premier League and now academy director at Fulham FC, this is a moral dilemma. 'You cannot put your head on the pillow at night in the knowledge that 80 per cent or more of young players aren't going to have football careers and that they might have been used as a commodity. If that is all you are doing at a football club, you won't succeed.

'I have had discussions with a number of parents in the past who have said their sons have benefited hugely during their time with us in terms of health, diet and nutrition, hydration and sleep patterns. These are lessons these kids will benefit from forever. I don't think we should fear having those as good targets and skills to utilise. We are very good at looking after boys, but not very good at saying so.'

We know that there are some good academies and centres of excellence and some bad ones. But how many clubs truly work with schools to help players they have released? As we have heard, sometimes they are barely willing to talk to the parents of the players they release, let alone agree to be party to a 'multi-agency approach' to the problem. Dave Woollaston of the English Schools FA and a schoolteacher in Luton is sceptical of the attitudes of most clubs, 'I'm lucky. I work in a good school where we can help, but some schools I know have had kids who have been difficult after they have been released. All they want to do is reach the age of 16 and leave, so they don't really give their full attention in school and when they are discarded by the clubs they fall heavily.

'Many clubs don't have any real strategies to help these boys back into normal society and they do go through a certain amount of trauma. Some clubs insist they have back-up plans – but I can say that in the ten years the system has been running with all the boys we have in academies and centres of excellence, not once have I had anyone from a professional football club come to me to discuss how they are getting on and how we can handle their exit strategy.'

So what are the alternatives?

In February 2004, Bob Marley, a director at non-League Worcester City at the time (he has since resigned), came up with a radical idea. He wanted to start a Midlands non-League club youth development league for 12- to 16-year-old players. 'We had a college scheme for our 16- to 18-year-old players at a local further education college,' Marley explained. 'But we want to develop our own players to feed into that.

'It was about meeting our community responsibilities as local clubs and finding a level of football that was better than Sunday afternoon junior football, but not as pressurised and demanding for the players as the Football League system,' he added.

The trouble is that non-League clubs are shafted when it comes to youth development. They are outside the compensation mechanism, which means professional clubs can come in and take the better players they have developed for free. So where is the incentive for them? Nonetheless the scheme had great merit. Marley wanted to lift his own club's youth teams out of the malaise of local junior league soccer. He had seen one of their under-16s stamped on during a game, 'I saw what had happened and realised that I didn't want to put boys representing the club in that kind of environment while I was a director of the football club. I knew I had to do something about it.'

The benefit of what became known as the Midland Junior Premier Football League (MJPFL) was that it was a new tier of football, sitting above local junior leagues, but a step down from the professional club academies. It was a regional solution – minimising the travel time boys spent reaching professional club centres to train. It was on their doorstep – and matches could be scheduled around the schools programme on Saturday mornings. 'Fellow non-League clubs in the Midlands saw its worth from the word go and have stayed involved ever since. Their support was fantastic,' said Marley.

Players could be recruited within the local community and many of them would probably be boys who had been rejected by professional clubs. It could be a classic 'safety net', offering them a good standard of football and the chance to turn their fledgling football careers around. If relationships were built between the participating clubs and the better junior clubs in their area, then some real development work within the junior pyramid could be built.

Within two months the league was launched with former England footballer Cyrille Regis on board as president – a player who fitted the role perfectly, as he had gone straight from non-League obscurity into the old First Division with West Bromwich Albion and enjoyed a 20-year professional playing career. While his appointment might not have meant much to many of the MJPFL players, their dads would certainly remember Cyrille's rags to riches rise, and he has turned out to be a tireless worker for the new league, as he spotted its potential from day one.

Matches began in September 2004, with just a dozen clubs on board with divisions for under-13s to under-16s. This has now stretched from under-12s to under-18s. Indeed for 2008-09, the MJPFL had 2,500 players registered in 108 teams representing 47 different non-League clubs, serving a huge geographical tract from the east Midlands to the south-west and Wales. Matches are split geographically to minimise travel time.

Bob Marley stepped down in 2007 after three years at the helm, handing the baton to Andy Barnett, the MJPFL's former secretary. During an interview for this book Barnett estimated that roughly one-third of the players in the league had been at professional academies or centres of excellence. He didn't know how many had turned their careers around and hopped back into professional club academies, but he said that 12 players had signed contracts at senior level, five had played international representative football and dozens were playing as semi-professionals in non-League football.

In short, the league is working. It is giving fresh opportunities to boys and is now an established part of the youth development picture. 'The boys are getting better coaching and the coaches are being offered better opportunities,' said Marley. 'I am delighted that the people who have taken it on are doing as good a job as they can with the time commitments they have got. It is unfortunate the FA can't find the funds to roll the system out nationally. It would be money well spent.'

Like Cirencester with the college academy, Watford with their educational link up with Harefield Academy, Manchester United insisting that four-a-side is best for the development of under-12s – the MJPFL is a branch of the youth game which has ploughed on, doing its thing, providing solutions to problems, and not waiting for the rusty old gears of the FA or the professional leagues to churn into action.

The MJPFL has come into existence without receiving a penny from the rest of the game and there is no financial reward whatsoever for anyone involved. It is doing what is best for the kids. Imagine how much more realistic it would be if the game's governors, instead of expecting Andy Barnett to put in 850 hours of free time around his career, were to provide a smidgen of the cash they are ladling out to professional clubs so the league could develop nationally and be put on a proper commercial footing, instead of being motored by goodwill.

When I first interviewed Nathan Wall and Ryan Craig in 2007, both were already playing in the MJPFL but I asked them to talk about their past experiences. When I met them again in January 2009, both boys had grown up considerably. Nathan was now a 17-year-old, six-footer, Ryan, just turned 13, still sounded angelically young, but by all accounts was making great strides as a footballer. Both had won MJPFL trophies – Nathan playing for Boldmere, Ryan for Redditch United. 'Being released from Walsall was a blessing in disguise,' is how Nathan's dad, Steven, now views things. 'I'm a lot happier,' said Nathan. 'I think in the professional game they just ask too much from you from too young an age. If I was going in now [at 17 years old] it would be right, but from nine years old it was too much.' And Ryan said of the MJPFL, 'I really like it – it is a good standard of football.' Dad Adrian added, 'He is getting his confidence back and is playing with a smile again.'

What a great story. How good must Bob Marley feel when he hears that the MJPFL has helped get cynical youngsters' appetites for the game back? 'No,' said Marley. 'The league we started didn't do it by itself, we were helped by those boys' mums and dads and all the other willing workers. It's about working together, isn't it?'

There are others, though, who say it's time to seize the game back for the benefit of all children.

CHAPTER 11

OI MISTER, CAN WE HAVE OUR GAME BACK?

Play is the universal language of children
Anon.

For too many years English football has worn its poor practices like some sort of badge of honour. At first-team level, managers and players are often allowed to set the worst possible examples of thuggish behaviour, whether it is on the pitch, on the touchline, on the training ground, in their cars, in pubs, in restaurants – anywhere. Too often, their clubs only grudgingly hand out fines, usually the bare minimum that is deemed socially acceptable. Reluctant to take coaching qualifications – the tools to learn how to do the job properly – too many coaches and managers want to get their feet under the gaffer's desk on the cheap.

The parents and coaches who prowl the touchlines of park's pitches often adopt the same caustic mannerisms as their counterparts at the top level, viewing almost every decision that goes against them as no less than an infringement of their human rights. It is small wonder that at some point there would be growing unease at the way children are treated within the professional game with its youth development programmes and the excesses in local grass roots junior football.

The two, of course, are linked. Let's face it; the English football industry has had an easy ride. For decades its clubs have revelled in the fact their young players were more likely to be graduates hauled up through the school of hard knocks rather than the school of science. For all the trawling, trading, culling, bawling and constant carping about pushy parents, the nightmares lurking within their own little dream factories have carried on unabated – divorced from reality.

'Do you know what it [grass roots football] is like?' bawled one of the interviewees during the research for this book, 'it's bloody awful.' But he was talking about what it was like 30 years ago when his kids played. For us ordinary recreational players who laced up their boots in, at best, wartime Nissen huts with no loos and ice cold showers. Behaviour-wise it has gotten worse. In 2005 I produced a programme for BBC Radio Five Live about violence in junior football. It presented a national snapshot at the time and revealed a number of horrific stories. For example, within recent months of that period someone had pointed a gun at a referee during a junior football match, and a parent had driven his son on to the pitch after a game and leapt out to try to knife the referee. Other referees had been spat at, kicked unconscious and a 15-year-old ref, officiating one of his first games, was repeatedly booted up the backside on his way back to the changing rooms by a pathetic bully of a parent. Five Live's email system crashed under the weight of listeners willing to share their experiences.

This is not all the fault of the professional game – but there are influencing factors. So yes, like millions of other people, unlike those cosseted within the world of professional football, I do know what goes on. However, it is important to remember that for all the 'bloody awful' incidents, there are many wonderful people who give their time for free, who love the game and sport in general, for what it is – fun. They realise that buried beneath the commercial dogma of football is a beautiful thing – a simple, wonderful sport. Someone has to stand up for it – otherwise there is no future.

Luckily, there are people who want to tell it how it is – no holds barred, to rage against the machine and shout, 'We've got to do something about it!'

In May 2006 Paul Cooper had one of those moments. A grass roots soccer coach and correspondent for *Soccer Coaching International* magazine, Cooper had finally had enough of the daft issues dominating junior coaching. He cracked. For years he hadn't liked what he had seen within junior football – the barking and bawling at children by coaches, the over-zealous parents, the lack of skills taught in the professional game, the undue seriousness at all levels, the drilling of little boys into teams and leagues, the overemphasis on winning – ugly aspects of the beautiful game.

The final straw was reading a comment from a head teacher who had said he wanted the best school team in the borough, so was after the best 11 boys he could find in the area. 'What about the other kids?' thought Cooper.

One day he wrote the headline for an article, 'Oh, For Christ's Sake, Just Give Us Back Our Game!' That was it, the clarion call. A campaign slogan, right on the money, doing what it said on the can. After all the game belongs to kids. 'That was the catalyst,' recalls Cooper. It rang a bell. For this to be more than the usual chivvy-up football industry talk about having fun (often used, as if just saying the words alone will do), it had to have substance.

'I contacted 20 to 30 people I had met on courses and in various other ways to see if they were interested,' recalls Cooper. One of the first people Cooper called was Rick Fenoglio, exercise and sports scientist at Manchester Metropolitan University, who worked with Manchester United to develop their four-a-side game. 'I'm in,' said Rick, who also persuaded Tony Whelan at Manchester United's academy to offer his support. Another early bird was Bert-Jan Heijmans, a Dutch coach living in the north-east of England. Officially the technical coordinator at Brandon FC, a small Durham-based club, he got in touch with Cooper to tell him about the Dutch-style coaching courses he ran, because Give Us Back Our Game (GUBOG) suited much, though not all, of the things he had been saying about the ineffective approach to developing young players for years.

Support also came from academic Dr Andy Pitchford, a lecturer in Sport and Exercise Science based at the University of Gloucestershire. Co-author of *Child Welfare in Football* (2006), he had closely studied some of the game's excesses in youth development. And author and children's campaigner Sue Palmer, author of *Toxic Childhood* (2006), a book about the influence of contemporary culture on children's development – particularly their capacity to learn – also became a GUBOG supporter.

This merry band, and other dissenting disciples who could see the emperor's new clothes of modern football coaching – so often adult-driven for its own glorification, but so often stifling enthusiasm, creativity and enjoyment – decided to shape a new philosophy. 'We started a website in October 2006, and it has grown ever since,' said Cooper.

GUBOG has no formal structure, you can't join and there is no committee. Instead Fenoglio describes it as 'a mission'. 'It conjures up this idea of adults stealing the game. It's bigger than football. It represents hope for children around the world to play, have fun, to be creative and healthy. It is about escaping the tyranny of bad policy and laziness.'

Give Us Back Our Game has fermented into a range of ideas and child-centred best practice, which is being delivered at coaching days and seminars and is charting quite a different course to the hothouse coaching of children in England's football academies. 'It will benefit them as children and, ultimately, the future of English football,' said Fenoglio.

At the heart of it is childhood and the importance of play ... not necessarily playing football ... just playing and developing a range of social and sporting skills. It seems too many people in the football industry are blinkered by the belief that the only possible *raison d'être* for children to slip on boots or pull a football shirt over their head is so they can become a professional player.

GUBOG has struck a chord. 'In the past two years we have had over 150 TV, radio, magazine and newspaper articles written about us,' said Cooper. 'We do workshops at grass roots clubs, local councils, schools and county FAs such as Somerset, Essex and Shropshire, who are taking up the Give Us Back Our Game philosophy'. They also run community coaching sessions. 'We did a massive one in Battersea Park and about 500 or 600 kids of mixed ages and abilities came from the local estates,' recalls Cooper. 'They refereed the games themselves and really enjoyed it.'

To the football business, of course, the values Give Us Back Our Game espouses are little more than heresy. 'Some like what we do, others think we are a threat,' said Cooper. However, its aims and values are worth a chapter in this book because, maybe, they provide answers to some of the problems English youth development is facing. It is challenging some of the floundering concepts that dominate much of professional football industry thinking which, driven relentlessly by money, is trawling for its talent as young as possible and handing that duty over to professional football club coaches whose primary interest and loyalty, when all is said and done, is to the club crest and their employers, and not necessarily to the child.

Cooper's ideas came mainly from his own experiences. Born in 1957, he had a typical British post-war childhood. Raised in North Devon, he recalls joyous times playing sport, mainly football, from dawn 'til dusk. 'Children don't need to be drilled,' explains Cooper. 'They should be allowed to play. What they don't need is pressure from adults ordering them what to do. If they love the game they will flourish as players. It shouldn't be just a means to an end.'

'It wasn't a hotbed of football. There was little in the way of street football, but we made our own entertainment,' explains Cooper. 'We played with other boys in the village and organised our own games. We made our own kit and our own goals. There was absolutely no adult involvement at all. I never had a referee until I was an adult. It was fantastic.'

It would be easy to dismiss this sort of thing as wistful 'jumpers for goalposts' memories from days gone by. But that was the way it was. Sport was to be enjoyed. A boy's first steps in playing football were not at an organised junior club with greasy mitted 'scouts' looking to usher you in the direction of a professional club if you could kick a ball half decently. Sport had its own reward – fun.

Cooper was nine years old when England won the World Cup. 'It was a great time to come of age football-wise,' said Cooper, who recalls cycling to Westward Ho beach to play other teams. 'You'd get the occasional fight, but the kids made it work by creating their own rules. The best players would pair off, and select the next best two and so on until you had two even teams. It that failed – if a team, say, was

5-0 up you'd swap a couple of players around to shape a competitive match. There were no 15-0 hammerings – or parents wanting to gloat about it in the local press.'

Same with older boys – Paul's brother was three years older than him and his pals. 'If we played with them, the older boys would agree only to use their left foot or to score only with their heads. We always tried to even it up – to keep it fun. People forget – kids want fun – and the best way to make it enjoyable is for it to be close and competitive. Sport was not about thrashing the opposition. That spirit has been lost – and we have to get it back.'

Socially, of course, this isn't easy today. There are more cars, fewer municipal pitches and less waste ground. The perils of drugs, gangs, knife crime and so on are very real, especially in urban areas. The easy option for children and their parents is to stay indoors where it is safe and warm, even at the risk of becoming couch potatoes, playing endlessly on PCs or games consoles.

There are some shocking statistics related to this inactivity according to research commissioned by health awareness groups and conducted by several British academic institutions. These include: more than one in four children watch in excess of three hours of television a day; on non-school days a majority of kids are glued to more than three hours of television, two hours watching DVDs and two hours playing computer games; 21 per cent of children don't take part in outdoor sports at all during their free time and 12 per cent of children spend no time playing outside with friends during the holidays and weekends.

Twelve year olds were found to be the least active: 52 per cent of them play less than an hour of outdoor sports each day over the weekends or holidays and 29 per cent of 12- to 15-year-olds spend absolutely no time at all playing outdoor sports. It is no wonder that the number of obese children in the UK has doubled in the last ten years and now stands at one in four.

Cooper's own playing career failed to progress past the Reading Combination Second Division, but his interest in coaching developed, like so many parents, when his son, Charlie, started playing football at six years old. Charlie was among the first batch of children to attend the new junior sessions that Cirencester Town were promoting in 1995 as part of their dual-pronged approach to developing young players – their academy on one hand and junior football on the other – in particular the new form of fun-based, seven-a-side football promoted by the FA – Mini Soccer.

Paul began to coach the Under-7s. 'There were no leagues, just home and away friendly matches,' recalls Cooper. 'We used cones to mark out the touchlines. The boys played two games a session so all the kids got a chance to play. It was all about fun.'

As a parent and coach, Cooper followed Charlie's progress through the various age ranges, so they left Mini Soccer behind. However, when he returned to Mini Soccer as a coach a few years later he couldn't believe what had happened. 'The leagues came in, and if you have leagues you have tables. If you have tables, you have results and so it is the results that begin to matter most,' argued Cooper. 'The FA introduced tighter rules. It was more organised and less about fun and participation. It was very regimented and adult-oriented.'

And there is the problem as Cooper sees it – adults. 'You have tracksuits with initials on; coaches acting like Premier League managers. Adults actually saw Mini Soccer the same way they saw the Premiership.'

Cue more shoulder-shrugging from the FA, who didn't seem to have anything to say on the matter. 'No one from the FA was telling them that this was wrong. This was a fun game they had designed and they weren't saying anything. It has become a complete lottery for kids regarding the quality of coaching they would receive if they started going to Mini Soccer sessions.'

And there's the rub. Sir Trevor Brooking would have had fewer problems rolling out his skills coaching to 5 to 11 year olds if the FA had held the line. Instead, they let Mini Soccer become, what Cooper calls 'adultified.'

Some of the instances he recalls seeing make him smile and shake his head at the same time: an assistant manager stood behind a goal telling his goalkeeper what to do the whole time; coaches running up and down the line, 'moving the players around like planes on a Battle of Britain tactical board'; and, in one game, when a team won a corner, a coach shouting 'wait' before walking up to the boy who was going to take it and telling him what to do. 'The boy was so flummoxed he just kicked the ball into touch,' laughed Cooper.

'The players are like puppets on a string. These little dots who still believe in Father Christmas and the Tooth Fairy are just pawns in a bigger game led by a coach who thinks he's Sir Alex Ferguson. It has got worse year-on-year. It is completely about the adults' aspirations, not the children who simply do what they're told.

'It has become regimented. There is, in effect, no difference between what is happening in the under-7s in a Mini Soccer league and what is taking place in the Premiership – squad sizes, league tables, referees, fines – all inappropriate stuff for kids who really just want to turn up and say "fancy a game?" A lot of boys walk away from football because it just isn't enough fun. There are too many experts on sport and play who are adults. Surely the experts on play are children?'

Cooper is equally dismissive of some of the measures aimed at curbing excessive behaviour. 'What the FA are doing with their 'Respect' campaign is accepting the problem. They are saying, "how can we manage it?" when they need to change it. Having taped-off areas for parents at matches is merely acknowledging their right to bawl and shout … but from a distance.'

He became disillusioned with English coaching methods, and looked further afield. 'The FA courses turned me off, so I started looking at what was going on in other countries, in particular Holland. I was interested in the ethos of players getting more touches, getting more involved in games, so they became better players and started to enjoy playing for playing's sake, not just as a means to an end.'

What he was learning, and the ideas being swapped between grass roots coaches on forums like 'Footy4Kids', and 'Half Time Talk', persuaded Cooper to call for a change in the culture of coaching junior football. 'We have to move to an environment where the kids have control. The most difficult thing for kids to do these days is just to have a game of football among themselves. Everything has to be organised and played as if it means something. Everything is dictated by adults. The training is adult-orientated – children don't have a voice.'

The answer, according to GUBOG, is simple – offer some quality coaching, but let the kids make up the rules for the games they want to play. In April 2007 GUBOG organised what they dryly called a one-day seminar at Repton School in Derbyshire. In reality, it was much more. Several professional club junior teams turned up to run taster sessions with dozens of coaches from all kinds of backgrounds, ranging from the pro game to education, keen to discover more about Give Us Back Our Game's aims. 'The one thing that struck me', said Cooper, 'was, not so much how quiet things were, far from it – the boys were noisy and boisterous – but how little instruction and intervention there was. Without having to constantly question whose throw in it was, the boys just got on with the games.'

'Most youth football is seven-a-side in leagues across the country – three points for a win, adulation for the winners and the winning coaches and derision for the losers,' said Rick Fenoglio. 'If you put anyone in that environment it is natural that they will play to win and so the problems we see emerge. It is not inherent in the people, it is inherent in the structure they are being asked to play in week-in, week-out.

'Changing the structure is the only way to gain back the game for what it is intended to be – and that is to develop good, healthy young people who enjoy sport.'

A big issue for Paul Cooper is the sadness he feels at seeing substitutes looking on from the sidelines, getting cold – indeed GUBOG's logo is accompanied by a photo of a child sat on a ball staring forlornly into the distance. 'Why do we have substitutes in children's football? The simple answer is that they are there in the adult game which we see on TV and adults think children's football should be the same', said Cooper.

A few days after the Repton event I went to Manchester United's training ground at Carrington. Tony Whelan, United's assistant academy director who runs their Under-9 to Under-16 programme, explained the club's response to over-coaching. 'If you asked all the great players down the years I am sure they will say they taught themselves to play,' said Whelan, a former United youth player. 'I think they learned mostly from watching their peers and the best players.

For kids here it will be a Wayne Rooney goal or something from Ronaldo that excites them. They want to go out and practise it. I think that's far more important than what a coach can offer.'

Whelan has introduced something called 'inquiry based learning', and the club works hard at creating a relaxed environment for the club's under-12s in particular. The coaching is based on sound educational principles ... and it's fun. 'If they enjoy the game they'll want to play it and they'll want to learn and practise away from the club,' said Whelan. 'This is fundamental for developing skills in an environment that is safe, that is non-threatening, that is player-centred. We believe the players should make their own decisions at a young age and learn that it's OK to make mistakes. Mistakes are an important stepping stone to learning.

'Remember when you were a young boy and your parents took you to a maze?' he asked. 'Imagine if they'd taken you to the centre and then led you out again. Where's the fun in that? The fun is the experience of getting lost and finding your way out. That is what coaching is – problem solving. We believe it's best for the players to solve their own problems. A football coach has a lot of power. He has the power to create, but also to destroy. We're trying to remove the fear factor from the boys.'

Watching some of the coaching taking place it is clearly fun. They are set little exercises and the coaches only intervene to adapt the rules, to challenge the boys by making things a bit tougher. Under-12s coach John Shiels explained a practice session he was doing. 'We're replicating a tight situation. They've got to think quickly, they've got to choose the right pass. They've got to communicate. It's fantastic.' He ends up on his backside, chasing the boys around. There are giggles all round.

'It's really good fun,' laughed one of the players. 'This is what it's all about,' says Shiels. 'These are expert under-12 players so if we give them a problem to solve they'll work it out for themselves – and if they work it out for themselves they'll be stronger for it – stronger than a coach telling them what to do. If they enjoy it, they learn it quicker, they'll retain it longer then they'll return with a smile on their face the next time. It's not work, its play.'

The Premier League academy games programme normally sets eight-a-side matches. But United have developed a four-a-side game, which the Premier League have allowed them to use for home matches only. Rick Fenoglio and a team of researchers at Manchester Metropolitan University observed the scheme in a pilot study between 2002 and 2004. 'They wanted to improve and develop their players so they decided to play four v. four games, which were designed to bring out different aspects of play such as switching play, dribbling and shooting,' explained Fenoglio. 'The games showed that the players more than doubled the amount of touches they would have got in an eight v. eight game, so it increased the actual amount of football play. It is refreshing. Kids want to play and the United pilot is about freeing them up to express themselves and that is what it did.

'In the first few months of the trial when they played away games against Premier League clubs, with eight-a-side, they invariably got beaten, but after six weeks or so they started to draw level and by the end of the season they were beating the other teams. The four-a-side matches not only helped their game, but it transferred over to their eight-a-side game, too.

'It gets back to core skill development – playing the game. If you ensure children are playing more they will improve faster and be better players. United looked at the barriers that got in the way of play and worked out how they could manipulate the environment to break down those barriers.'

This is something that the Give Us Back Our Game programme has also done. If you reduce the pitch size and the number of players, you are going to have more play. The combination of the right environment and the reduced number of players allows real skill development and optimisation.

'It's not rocket science, is it?' said Tony Whelan. No, but if it's good enough for Manchester United, then surely it's good enough for any club. Only time will tell if United's young players who have been schooled in their fun four-a-side games will make the grade. But Paul Cooper believes it can only help, 'We have too many players that are one-dimensional. We have a huge amount of excellent raw talent in England. Children want to use their creativity and imagination, but a lot of them are not getting through so something must be going wrong.'

At the other end of the football scale sits Storm FC, a junior club based in South Norwood in south London. One of their coaches, Vanessa Wheeler, faced a familiar problem in grass roots junior football. Along with a number of other players her son, Haydn, hadn't quite made it into the Storm Thunder Under-9s team. The Wheeler family faced a dilemma – whether to allow Haydn to spend a season on the sidelines, to search for another club or to give up the game altogether.

Vanessa decided to set up a new team, Storm Lightning, for fringe players and new recruits. Trouble is, she couldn't decide which league to put them into. Most of the players were keen on their football, but weren't that good so she feared they might get tonked every week. Could they balance players between Storm Thunder and Storm Lightning? But then what do you do about players being registered to play for one team or another? Confused, she called Paul Cooper for advice. 'Why play in a league at all,' was his reply. 'Just play practice matches with both teams.' Cooper was spot on.

For Radio 4 I went down to South Norwood to do a feature on this unusual junior team that plays no matches. Vanessa was a wonderful host and the club was a fantastic little community venture. Without the burden of matches, the involvement and enjoyment was palpable. They simply split into teams and played their own mini-tournament of short-sided, five-minute-long matches. Every player got lots of touches, had a laugh and developed their skills in a close-knit environment. The tournament was done and dusted within two hours. The kids loved it, so did the parents and there was no antagonism from the sidelines. Indeed, all the parents seemed supportive and accommodating.

If those children had been put into a team that played in a league and was losing each week, would many of them have stayed? Probably not. Two years on and both teams are still going – it's a minor success story. Who says it is all about results?

Paul Cooper runs his own community coaching scheme in Cirencester. Again there are no results and no teams – just lots of kids of different abilities and different ages, mixed in, having fun. The younger ones learn the rudiments, the older ones share the ball around. It attracts over 100 kids in the summer and smaller groups in the winter months.

The striking thing is that the kids make up the rules – they lay the ground rules and don't bother with throw-ins or other time-wasting paraphernalia. They just get on with the game. Every so often the bigger ones have to freeze so the little ones can get the ball and get some shots in. 'It's not considered very PC,' says Cooper, 'We have boys of seven playing with 13 year olds. Why? Because it's fun – you're not supposed to have that anymore because you have to play with children of your own age, but we encourage them to make up the rules so brothers and sisters or differing ages can play together.'

Cooper recalls the police turning up to one of the sessions. 'They said, "Since you've been doing this youth crime in the area has gone down by 70 per cent." They are all local kids – they are getting an extra four hours a week of parks football. The social implications with this are huge. We had one seven-year-old kid come along who was massively overweight. When he first came he didn't want to talk or get involved, but now he is more confident and his social skills are better, he is slowly losing weight and is more active.

'They have to get involved because they work it out for themselves. The most awkward boys are the ones that have been at football academies because they have been told "you're the best" and they are sometimes too cocky.

'We have seen from Give Us Back Our Game events that children play completely differently when they are on their own to when adults are involved,' says Cooper. 'Sometimes we have to step in to sort out arguments – that is inevitable – but it doesn't often happen. Kids are great at making the rules work for them – adults forget that. We were all kids like that once.

'We want to stage Give Us Back Our Game street-football sessions in every town in England, so we can offer free football 46 weeks of the year for an average of three hours per week for any age.' The trouble is that Give Us Back Our Game has very little money. 'We get small grants from local funding groups, but it is a struggle,' admits Cooper. 'It is difficult for us to get financial support because much of what we do is classified as "play" rather than "sport".'

Nonetheless the initiative is gaining momentum. In January 2009, Cooper made a keynote speech at a two-day English Golf Union conference called, appropriately enough, 'Give Us Back Our Game'. 'I have only ever played crazy golf on the seafront at Bognor Regis so it was interesting – but it shows they are having issues in other sports too,' added Cooper. In the same month it was announced that research projects at the Department of Exercise and Sport Science at Manchester Metropolitan University (MMU) and the Faculty of Sport, Health and Social Care at the University of Gloucestershire will be launched, based on the issues raised by Give Us Back Our Game.

It is envisaged that the GUBOG Centre at MMU will undertake academic research in youth sport participation and retention and will co-ordinate future Give Us Back Our Game coaching and educational programmes, with the first GUBOG conference being held there in September 2009. The GUBOG Centre at the University of Gloucestershire will deliver focussed football sessions with the GUBOG ethos for young players on weekends and co-ordinate under-graduate student volunteers and training. Andy Pitchford, the University of Gloucestershire's deputy head of department, said, 'The philosophy of Give Us Back Our Game and its child-centred approach fits comfortably with our university's strategic policies of widening participation and community work.'

The campaign has also gone global – Give Us Back Our Game coaching sessions have been staged in 15 countries including the United States, Canada, Australia, New Zealand, Sweden, the Philippines (where 700 players attended a GUBOG day in Manila – the biggest event so far), India, Finland and Poland. In February 2009 the initiative launched its own quarterly publication – in conjunction with *Soccer Coach International* magazine.

Closer to home in Cirencester, at the end of the indoor session, Paul had been taking the overweight seven year old – who had struggled with his self-esteem – fishing a ball out of the bag, placing it carefully on the ground and very deliberately starting to practise a step over and one or two other moves. A few months ago the boy had barely kicked a ball in anger – now he wants to learn to do it with finesse. It will hopefully be a life-long journey for him. By now all the other kids had disappeared. His grandmother breezes in, 'How many goals this week?' she jokes. None again – but he's getting better and has the ball at his feet, and has had plenty of touches. He's getting the game back from those who would cast him to one side. Good lad.

This is a world away from England's elite academies. In other countries there isn't the huge gap between this sort of community football project and coaching at local professional clubs. It is more structured, more streamlined, and some might say, more successful.

CHAPTER 12

IN OTHER SPORTS AND ON FOREIGN FIELDS

One of the often-repeated myths of youth development in England is that the new system is trying to copy what goes on in other leading European football countries – that somehow the English game is playing catch up with those clever continentals and that we are steadily improving the way young footballers are developed. On the continent (the theory goes) they manage to 'get hold' of kids at young ages and 'work them'. It is said they 'work the 5 to 11 years olds' particularly well.

Our problem, the thinking goes, is that we just don't have the same 'access time'. So along comes the academy system, designed to allow professional clubs greater access to children.

However the problem is less to do with access time, but more that the professional English clubs have little interest in national football development. At the top end of the game, English clubs – often owned by international businessmen – are increasingly driven by self-interest. They want to 'have access' to younger and younger players so that they can 'work them' to achieve success for their club. They do not see the well-being of the nation's sporting youth as one of their main priorities.

Dave Parnaby at Middlesbrough recalled that during a visit to Vitesse Arnhem FC in Holland he asked a coach how they were doing. 'Very nicely, thank you,' was the reply. What Dave meant was to ask how the *club* was doing; the coach assumed that he was talking about the Dutch football system. 'He spoke in a national sense rather than about his own club,' said Parnaby. 'That is how they see the technical aspects of their programme – in a national framework. That is why Holland has one of the best reputations for youth development in Europe.

'The fact is that everyone in England should feel part of the youth development programme, from children's teams right up to Steven Gerrard and the like stepping out for England. So when you are watching England on TV and they are losing to Croatia – and you're throwing your slippers at the telly or whatever – you are part of the team and can ask yourself, "What part did I play in that?"'

But England is a club country. Many fans support their club teams first and foremost and will defend them to the hilt. It's not that they don't care about the England national team or the wider good of the game in principle, but the notion of a collectivist national pro-gramme of development flies out of the window when subjects such as the 'need' for clubs to sign the best players – no matter how they achieve it – crops up. The notion of 'losing' players – to England representative squads is a club perspective and takes no account of what might be best for the player's development or indeed that of the national team.

No matter how educated and thoughtful they may be, when it comes to their football clubs many football supporters don't care *how* young players come into their club, just so long as they continue to do so and that they are the best. Period. Of course, this is not true of all supporters – and many clubs have quite progressive policies in terms of community awareness and youth development – but, broadly speaking, it is a truism.

Even worse is that despite the reorganisation brought about by Howard Wilkinson's *A Charter for Quality* we are not catching up with other countries like Holland. Instead English football is allowing its clubs to trawl for future football talent for their own private gain, with no central authority in charge of 'the system'. Just listen to the vitriol aimed at the FA for trying to maintain a grip on the youth development tiller. The leagues, made up of member clubs, see the FA as a one-third 'stakeholder.' In essence, English football is taking tiny pieces of a jigsaw puzzle, getting them wrong, and trying to make them fit a bigger picture. But the image has ended up looking grotesque. What is needed is a national policy for change – a complete change of tack, which isn't just about football but also involves mainstream education. This simply will not happen if matters are left up to the clubs who, by nature, protect their own interests.

Let's get back to Holland. Everyone seems to agree that it is the clever old Dutch who seem to have got it right. It might seem strange to investigate the matter by watching the junior section of Brandon FC, a team from the north-west of England, being put through their paces on an Astroturf pitch on a bitterly cold Friday evening. But this is where Bert-Jan Heijmans, a UEFA A qualified coach and all-round football enthusiast known as 'BJ', has chosen to ply his trade. He has lived in the UK since 1997, when he moved here to work as a pharmaceutical engineer while his wife Anna worked as a psychology professor at the University of Teesside.

They settled in Brandon, a village a few miles south of the city of Durham. BJ describes himself as an 'extreme coach'. Has something been lost in translation? No, he says; it means he thinks outside of the box and is therefore seen as a slightly threatening figure in the rigid-thinking confines of English football coaching. 'Extreme in England, not in Holland,' is how he clarifies things.

BJ has occasionally stirred things up in England. He has irritated junior leagues through his desire to play games with rush-back goalkeepers. The leagues argue that too many goals will be scored. BJ's tack is, 'so what?' He would prefer to see everyone getting involved. Having two goalkeepers means two boys are missing out on playing football in the middle.

Having ditched his chemistry career, BJ also runs coaching courses throughout Britain and is considered to be something of a colourful character. I have hotfooted it here from meeting Dave Parnaby at Middlesbrough. When he asked who I was meeting next and I told him it was Heijmans, he pointed to my recorder and said, 'Oh dear. I hope you've got plenty of spare tape, because you're going to need it.'

During my visit BJ is keeping an eye on his team of coaches, who are putting some of the club's 200 junior players through their paces. It is an impressive number for an English junior village club, but would be considered quite small in Holland. However, BJ is slightly grouchy. He bemoans the lack of a clubhouse on such a cold winter's night – par for the course in his homeland. 'English clubs never have clubhouses. It should be the heart of the club. It is where you develop spirit and exchange ideas. Everyone will trudge off home tonight after training– no unity will have been built.'

He tut-tuts as he spots a coach laying out a wavy line of cones for a drill. All the time he emphasises the need for boys to have as many touches of the ball as possible. It is all about the ball. He wants them to run with it, to get used to dribbling. He wants them to practise a range of passes – short and long – moving, thinking, engaging with the game. BJ loves the pace and passion of English football, its competitiveness – arguably its most alluring appeal – and its traditions, but he is a harsh critic overall.

Brandon United was originally formed as a Sunday morning side called Rostrons, a waste paper company where most of the founding players worked when they began playing in the Durham and District Sunday League in 1968-69. Today, the club's first team competes in the Northern League Division Two – though financially, it is a struggle. Their high points have been two FA Cup-first round appearances.

Keen to help his local club, Heijmans got involved several years ago and has developed a coaching strategy at Brandon. What he has seen in England shocks him. It is a far cry from his upbringing in the town of Rosmalen in southern Holland where the local football club, and others like it, are genuinely at the hub of the local community. Heijmans even knows of a Dutch village of 1,600 people where 500 are members of the local football club. 'That doesn't happen in England'.

BJ feels youth development in England is dominated by age-old thinking. He is an advocate of Give Us Back Our Game, but only so far – he isn't altogether convinced that if you overemphasise fun and play you will be taken seriously. He runs coaching tours to Holland from England – for disciples who are eager to learn to coach the Dutch way – taking in experiences at small and large clubs, coaching seminars and watching games. The Dutch clubs they visit are at the heart of their communities – even the big clubs Ajax, Feyenoord or PSV have links with smaller clubs. It is a co-ordinated approach with joined-up thinking. 'Coaching is a profession,' says BJ, 'something to be proud of, not something to avoid as managers often do here.'

He is wary of counter criticism. If the Dutch are so great, why are they not dominating world and European football? 'We lose all our players and coaches abroad,' he says, but confesses that actually, at times Dutch football can be a bit too technical. But then the population of the Netherlands is only 16 million (the UK is 60 million, Germany 82 million, Italy 59 million and France 65 million) – i.e. roughly a quarter of the size of those countries – but nonetheless, it is considered to be successful on the international stage.

To understand the difference between English and Dutch football, let's have a closer look at Heijman's home-town team, OJC Rosmalen. The club is based in Rosmalen, a small town with a population of 35,000 in the southern province of North Brabant, and has played in the Hoofdklasse since 1998. This is the highest league level for amateur clubs in Holland – the equivalent in England of a lower-Football League club. Their high points have been winning the Dutch amateur cup in 1991 and 2000.

Their stadium, built in 2005, is called Sportpark De Groote Wielen. The club has nine pitches including five match pitches, two with floodlights and four floodlit training pitches. In total it has 22 sets of dressing rooms, 1,600 club members and 976 youth players. An amazing 100 teams play at 11-a-side, 7- and 4-a-side matches from under-5s to over-50s, including girls and women's teams, each weekend. The whole operation is run by 400 volunteers mostly made up of the club's 2,000 parents, who are described as the 'the engine of the club'.

OJC Rosmalen does, indeed, have a clubhouse – a rather large one – where it runs an after school club. Indeed, junior players go straight from school to training. There are great links with local schools whose staff ensure the youngsters get there safely. A club board is in charge of various arms of the business, including finance, administration, football and youth sections, and organises a wide range of fundraising activities, a community programme and other events and services. As reward for their efforts, volunteers are allowed free entry to first-team matches, given Christmas gifts and offered other incentives.

The club is an intrinsic part of the local community and is linked to the national football programme. In youth development, players move up and down through the programme – with clubs having formal links with the larger clubs. Ajax, for example, has three feeder clubs in Holland, and others around the world in South Africa, the United States and China.

Although the FA has tried to stimulate similar interest by kite-marking Charter Standard clubs, there are few comparisons in the UK. Indeed, even though English clubs can have academies overseas, they cannot enter formal links with clubs in their own country – so there isn't a direct structure that allows boys to get a good grounding at grass roots and progress upwards. In fact, there has been uproar when-ever it has been attempted, even though – with English home-grown players at Premier League clubs in particular struggling to get first-team experience – formal links with smaller clubs would be a good way of helping their development. Without a structure, by nature, the programme has to be piecemeal – it is often driven by smaller clubs having influential contacts at larger clubs rather than a fully prepared plan shaped with the players' development at heart.

'We have got to be more creative than the way we are at the moment,' urges Howard Wilkinson. 'Why can't the 18- to 21-year-old players, who are lacking opportunities at Premier League level, play for clubs in League One and Two who are struggling on gates of 2,000 to 4,000? I know from anecdotal evidence that smaller clubs would welcome partnerships with larger clubs which you see elsewhere in the world – where players are on long-term loans,' he added. 'It needs some structural change. In France it isn't a problem – their best players get opportunity. In Spain and Italy they farm them out to sister clubs.

'When I was a director at Notts County [between 2004 and 2007] I said to the board, "If I can secure an agreement with a Premier League club who would put up resources and guarantee to loan a number of players to the club each season, and would provide a coach to work on the development of the players would they be in favour?" The unanimous answer was "yes".'

It isn't just the football development structures that mark the gap between English football and its continental counterparts. It is also high-quality coaching. The reason top Dutch clubs, for example, trust their grass roots clubs to develop players is that they know the coaches will be highly qualified and will know how to coach properly. The numbers of such coaches in equivalent population countries simply dwarf those in English football – a point acknowledged in the FA's coaching strategy report for 2008 to 2012.

Let's take the top three coaching badges which have been standardised by European football's governing body UEFA and progress from UEFA B, to UEFA A and the Pro Licence (the top coaching qualification). In 2008 there were 1,759 UEFA B qualified coaches in England. In Spain the figure was 9,135. In France it was 15,000, Italy 27,430 and Germany 28,400. At UEFA A level in England we have a mere 895 qualified coaches. In Italy there are 1,298, France 2,400, Germany 5,500 and Spain 12,720. At Pro licence level, 115 English coaches have passed this very high level qualification. In France there are 188, Italy 512, Germany 1070 and Spain 2140.

It isn't hard to deduce where the coaching culture is more deeply ingrained. The FA's coaching targets are modest: to train another 2,500 at UEFA B, 100 at UEFA A licence, and 40 at the Pro Licence level by 2012.

In the meantime, England will slide further behind other European countries. But the grim reality is that at all levels of the game in England becoming a qualified coach is seen as something that you don't really have to do. How many top managers, who are either scooping large salaries or are about to, go bellyaching to their mates in the press about the rigors of having to be qualified, and try to wriggle around it? Just look at academies, where a temporary 18-month dispensation to allow time for coaches to get appropriately qualified so they continue to work in elite youth development instead became a standard gap, until coaches were eventually dragged by the ear kicking and screaming to their nearest course.

Despite a few improvements, the fact is that English football lacks an ingrained coaching culture. It's ridiculous, because better-quality coaches, working as part of a national network of grass roots clubs situated close to schools and involved with the local community, but feeding into professional clubs, could deliver the 10,000 hours of long-term elite athlete development 'Pitch to Podium' training that the country's top footballers need. As it is, most young players don't get anywhere close to those hours because they have to wait until 6 p.m. to start training at elite facilities miles away in the countryside, divorced from the rest of the game.

The logic, it seems, is driven by free market enterprise. So, let's look at how they develop sports stars in the world's top free market – the United States, the 'land of the free'. Dr Ralph Rogers is a sports medic who was born and raised in the US but has trained and practised in his homeland, in Europe and in the UK, where he now works as a team physician for the FA's England Under-16 and Under-19 youth teams, among many other roles in sport. He explained how athletes in the major US sports – American football, basketball and baseball – are prepared for their careers. 'Ninety to 95 per cent of them develop through high school, university and, then, the professional game,' he says. 'At school, you develop as an athlete – you are not being looked at by professional sports and you don't specialise in one particular sport.'

This stands in stark contrast to English football clubs who look to develop boys at six years of age or younger. 'You won't have, for example, the Dallas Cowboys or the New York Yankees going after five- or six-year-old kids,' said Dr Rogers. 'It just won't happen. There are strict rules and regulations to prevent that happening.'

The main difference is that the clubs are just not interested in doing it. They prefer to let the education system and grass roots clubs do it for them. 'You will get Mighty Mite clubs [recreational US sports teams at junior school level] working with kids and developing good clubs with facilities to a very high standard. Sport is a big part of US culture and they spend a lot of money on it,' said Dr Rogers.

'Because of the different sports seasons you can have exceptional athletes competing in three different sports to a very high standard at junior high school all year round. Specialisation won't happen until a player is 14 or 15 years old and ready to go to high school. That is when someone will gravitate towards a specific sport, such as basketball, for example.'

So let's make it clear: talented athletes up to 14 or 15 years old are still allowed to play a variety of sports. Private clubs are not allowed to do what many English football clubs do – tell their signed players that they cannot play other sports.

'High school sport is where it takes off,' says Dr Rogers. 'It is major; there is the tradition of school pride and winning. The locker rooms would rival a lot of professional club locker rooms I have seen in this country. You will get 10,000 to 15,000 people watching matches – those schools represent towns or districts in the same way that football clubs represent their communities in the UK – only they're not professional clubs – they are schools.'

What about at university and other education from the age of 18 upwards? 'That's when the real fun begins,' laughs Dr Rogers. 'That is when the big recruiting starts to take place.' But let's make it clear here that unlike their poor English counterparts studying leisure and tourism, these students are taking part in real education, at degree level. 'Parents in the US are wary that even at this advanced stage, there is a very small percentage chance their son will make it in professional sport. So the education is important. These are not lip service courses; they are full degree courses. They want their kid to be educated over that four years so he or she can get a decent job.'

So, even if you're not academically gifted, you still go to college? 'Absolutely,' says Dr Rogers. 'You have to pass an aptitude test to get in and if you don't achieve certain grades you will get thrown off the team and the sports staff can't do anything about it.'

In the US, college sport has enormous value in its own right. 'The amount of money they make from TV revenue is huge,' said Dr Rogers. 'At Michigan State you can get 100,000 every week to watch [American] football or 20,000 to watch basketball.' Who watches? 'Everyone – from alumni to the average man in the street even if they never went to university.'

As a result the sports facilities are first class. 'Unbelievable. The best you can ever imagine are there,' insists Dr Rogers. 'The finest coaches too. Well-educated coaches – guys who know how to manage people.'

So at what stage do professional clubs come in? 'They will be looking at the best freshmen (first-year students), but I would say 95 per cent of players see their college education through. They will have plenty of time to make it if they are good enough.'

Even then clubs cannot just waltz in and pick the best players. Instead, they have to go through a process called 'the Draft'. 'You are rated when you come out of college – you have to go through a series of physical tests – and depending on how you do, you are ranked in order,' explains Dr Rogers.

'The Draft is shown live on TV. The weakest team [the team that finishes at the foot of the table] gets the best draft choice, unless they sell that chance on to another club. What that means is that the best young players will, for a season at least, be with the weakest team, so that gives them a lift. The idea is that it prevents the creation of dynasties. You'll always have dominant teams, but it isn't like soccer in England, for example, where the same few clubs win all the trophies.'

US sports also have salary caps, which enable smaller clubs to compete with the bigger clubs. 'It gives everyone a chance and the fans enjoy that. They don't want to see the same few clubs competing at the top level all the time.' Again, it is structured, it is unified and it produces amazing athletes. They would think any other system was bizarre.

But what about other UK sports – how do they run their elite academy systems? There are few comparable examples to football because of the sport's popularity in England – but maybe the closest is rugby union which, since the sport turned professional in 1995, has formed its own Premiership, which has negotiated its own TV deal and has a brief legacy of flexing its muscles to shrug off impositions of the game's governing body, the Rugby Football Union (RFU).

Stuart Lancaster was appointed head of elite player development for the RFU in June 2008, and is head coach of England Saxons (effectively the national team's second string). A former PE teacher and player with Leeds Carnegie, his career was ended by injury at the age of 30 in 2000. In September 2001 he became the club's first academy manager, a role he retained until 2005 when he progressed to director of rugby. Then he moved on to his role at the RFU.

Academies were introduced into rugby union in 2001 after a funding deal was agreed with Sport England. Elite clubs were asked to submit bids to run academies under licence from the RFU for an initial eight-year period. Leeds was one of the first clubs to meet the criteria to run an academy programme. There are now 14 English rugby academies at each of the 12 Guinness Premiership clubs plus [at the time of writing] two National League clubs, Leeds Carnegie and Exeter.

In essence the system is similar to football. Clubs can register players and take them on full-time aged 16, balancing their rugby training with the Apprenticeship in Sporting Excellence (ASE) education programme. There is a compensation system to sort out squabbles if a player chooses to move from one club to another during the window of opportunity between 1 April and 31 July.

However, there are some tangible differences. For starters, clubs cannot sign players under the age of 13. The compensation fees are set at a fixed tariff of £10,000 per year, but only for 16- to 20-year-old players. Although at first the clubs were allowed unfettered access to players from anywhere in the country, the sport quickly learned its lessons. A new rule was introduced allotting each club a defined geographical county from which it could sign players. 'There was a lack of trust [before the new rule was introduced] and so there was no shared best practice among academies,' recalls Lancaster. 'The new rule has brought integrity to the system, because clubs are sticking with their patch as opposed to nicking everyone else's players.' It also means clubs are not driving down the age at which they seek to recruit youngsters. The players are allowed to play for their school and/or local junior clubs and only attend the academy for training. 'There is a good relationship between local schools and clubs,' explains Lancaster. 'They don't resent boys playing at an academy because they get him back to play for their clubs.'

Lancaster admitted that restricting the number of academies to 14 has been contested, with universities, in particular, keen to get on board. The RFU academy licences are reviewed on an annual basis and subject to an audit. In January 2009 one club out of the 14 that run academies was struggling to meet its required terms and conditions and if it failed to meet the RFU action plan by July 2009 it was to be put on notice – which meant the possibility of having its licence withdrawn.

The RFU provide funds worth £114,000 per academy per season, with clubs adding their own money. Lancaster estimated that the most expensive academy costs about £500,000 a year to run.

Elite players from the regional club academies go to the national academy and play for England squads – so there is a clear pathway leading from the grass roots to the pinnacle of the game. I asked Lancaster if he thought they could spot talented rugby players at pre-teen ages? 'I am not so sure you can, to be honest. You can identify all-round talent, but there are so many factors in between it isn't worth trying to recruit them.'

As a former teacher, like so many other educationalists, he can't understand football's obsession with early specialisation in the sport. 'If you look at the fundamentals of long-term player development, sports like football and rugby are supposed to be late specialist sports. It isn't good to focus solely on them when you are too young. What annoyed me when I was a PE teacher was that football clubs denied players the chance to play other sports. That happened all the time. Football academies turn around and say, "don't play for your school and don't play any other sport".'

So let's look at how it works at a specific club. In January 2007 I visited Collin Osborne, who was academy director at Harlequins at the time. He has since moved on to the role of first-team assistant coach at the club. Their training ground in Roehampton is a no-frills working environment. Harlequins have spent their money trying to achieve results rather than presenting an impressive facade.

The club's geographical patch, defined by the RFU, from which they are allowed to recruit their players is Sussex and Surrey. Even though there are four Premiership clubs in the south-east of England – Harlequins, Wasps, Saracens and London Irish – none of these clubs are allowed to encroach on each others counties for their talented young players. Harlequins have two development centres – one at their HQ at Roehampton in Surrey (in south-west London) and at Brighton in Sussex on the south coast. Both centres are designed to develop the best school-age rugby talent across the counties.

Osborne explained how players are encouraged to play for their local clubs and regional representative teams, but receive coaching from the professional academy – with the best players having the option of joining the academy full-time at 18.

He recalled it was a far cry from the 'bun fights' that occurred at the major youth festivals, before this system was devised, when coaches would attempt to woo players and their parents towards their club. 'It was crazy,' recalled Osborne. 'We used to have boys travel down from Nottingham, passing good clubs like Leicester and Northampton to reach us. Madness.'

The Harlequins Academy has roughly 100 boys in its schoolboy programme and 12 full-time scholars. 'Many are called, few are chosen,' said Osborne. 'We go for quality, not quantity.'

He said that Harlequins effectively matched from their own resources the £114,000 grant they received annually from the RFU to run the academy. Aside from two full-time academy coaches they had part-time specialists in physiotherapy, nutrition, psychology, welfare and technical skills and a further 12 part-time coaches.

In what Osborne described as a 'win-win situation', the boys play for their local clubs but train at the academy where they receive three specialist strength and conditioning training sessions plus a rugby skills coaching session per month. The club also invites them for extra training during school holidays.

This co-ordinated approach isn't currently possible in English football, because club academies can select from anywhere within the travel radius rules rather than limited defined geographical boundaries. It is, of course, more complicated. There are, after all, 92 professional Premier/Football League clubs – how would you divide their geographical recruiting boundaries? The clubs wouldn't accept it – but they could be compelled to work together – developing Howard Wilkinson's idea of smaller clubs linking formally to larger ones and down to the grass roots on a local and regional basis, with the top clubs coming in at the finishing stages of development and the FA (as they used to do) providing regional coaching centres. But any such model isn't on the agenda. The clubs have to adhere to academy and centre of excellence rules, but any idea of joined-up thinking is just not being applied, despite the problems facing the system.

The FA's coaching strategy report for 2008 to 2012 talks about putting the National Football Centre (NFC) at the heart of its plans as 'the hub of training and the development of excellence', and the home of Club England international teams – and having it open by 2011.

The FA board had given approval to proceed with the site at Burton-upon-Trent in May 2008 – but at the time of writing this book plans had still not been submitted to East Staffordshire Borough Council to restart building work.

The FA has already spent £28 million on the site and will need to stump up another £60 million to complete the project, which was mothballed as the FA ploughed on relentlessly with taking ownership of Wembley Stadium and rebuilding it, on which it has to meet the mortgage payments to cover the £400 million it has borrowed. In short, it opted for trying its hand at stadium management (it didn't own or manage the 'old' Wembley, which was in private hands), in preference to developing the national game and its much-vaunted 'hub'.

There is talk of the NFC rivalling Le Centre Technique National Fernand-Sastre at Clarefontaine in France. Throughout world sport the word 'Clairefontaine' is synonymous with excellence. The FA want 'Burton' to have the same profound impact on the English game and the same worldwide reputation. Not if it doesn't get built, it won't.

Meanwhile, other sports, which can't remotely match English football's revenue streams, have managed to build their elite national academies. The English Cricket Board (ECB) opened their National Academy at Loughborough University in October 2003, which has since been renamed the National Cricket Performance Centre (NCPC).

The NCPC is much more than just a training centre for England's Performance Programme players – it provides an all-year-round facility to benefit cricket as a whole. Its philosophy has been to identify the country's most talented cricketers and develop them through quality coaching, support services and outstanding facilities.

The NCPC facility is also a training base for all the ECB representative age-group teams, senior and junior England Women's squads – plus a base for development, coaching and rehabilitation programmes. It cost £4.5 million to build the indoor cricket centre, which has become the cornerstone of the development of England's young cricketers.

It has been built in partnership with Loughborough University, which has its own range of world-class training, medical and sports science facilities as part of the English Institute of Sport, which means that England's elite cricketers work alongside many of the country's best athletes from several other sports.

The NCPC has a 70m x 30m hall including six net lanes with full run-ups and space for the wicketkeeper to stand back from the wicket, high-tech filming and analysis resources and a performance analysis room. It also boasts a fitness and rehabilitation centre, fully equipped medical room, open-plan office and meeting room, seminar rooms and a player education room and dining area. Outside there is Loughborough University's main cricket ground, plus a bank of 18 grass nets and accommodation on-site. It is a true national centre of coaching.

Other British sports have similar national centres – such as British cycling's HQ at the Manchester Velodrome, the National Sailing Academy at Weymouth and the Lawn Tennis Association's National Tennis Centre at Roehampton in south-west London. Only football – the richest and most high profile sport of them all by miles – is rudderless when it comes to having its own nerve centre.

In the gas and oil funded super-rich Middle East, where money is no object, the emphasis up to now has been to build extravagant sports facilities as a means of attracting sports tourists and also to gain a foothold on world sport tournament circuits, rather than to cultivate their own domestic sporting talent. But some countries are changing tack and starting to invest heavily in salubrious sports centres to develop their own youth.

The world's biggest indoor multi-sports centre isn't in Europe, America or Far East Asia, but in the tiny gulf state of Qatar, a country with a population of roughly 1 million. 'Aspire today, inspire tomorrow,' is the slogan at Aspire, the handsomely state-funded, biggest sports academy in the world, with its unique blue-coloured dome – one half covering the most elaborate open-plan indoor sports facilities in the world, the other half housing Aspire's multi-sport academy, which is adjacent to the national Khalifa Stadium, and has recruited top coaches and physicians from around the globe.

Aspire is a long-haul view. In the most intense screening programme of its kind, every Qatari child has been assessed to see if they might benefit from joining Aspire full-time between the ages of 12 and 16 years. Although it only opened in 2004, Aspire's footballers are already holding their own against top European clubs like Benfica, Real Madrid, Arsenal and Bayer Leverkusen, and although this has been partly achieved by offering scholarships to non-Qataris, there is no doubt they are playing catch up – physically (Qatar's children are often smaller than their European counterparts) and in terms of technical ability.

Aspire's head football coach, Michael Browne, was employed by Charlton Athletic before landing this dream job. He told me their footballers were making rapid progress. The main problem was motivation – the boys who come here are the children of parents who, per head of population, are the richest in the world so it's not like they need to scrap to earn a living from the beautiful game – and most Qataris have little interest in their own domestic league. They prefer – surprise, surprise – the Premier League.

Nonetheless, Aspire is developing Qatar's home-grown talent in the best imaginable facilities. The theory is that football in Qatar may need home-grown stars to flourish and help to put it on the world sporting map. They are bidding to stage future Olympic Games and football World Cups. They have the infrastructure to do it tomorrow – much of it built to stage the 2006 Asian Games. Qatar took the gold medal in the Games' football tournament – which is effectively an under-23's competition. An amazing achievement, given that its tiny population is dwarfed by massive Asian countries like China, India and Japan.

Building up home-grown talent just seems the right thing to do, although screening an amazing 700,000 African children for just 23 places on Aspire's football programme in 2007 does seem well over the top.

Even here in the desert sun, where it is pointless attempting outdoor exercise for large parts of the day as temperatures can soar to 50°C and over, and where there is no ingrained sports culture, they understand the value of sports development and the need to have facilities and a structure to enable that to grow. Aside from its elite athlete work, Aspire also does outreach work to foster an interest in sport among pre-school children and women, who have, to put it mildly, not been encouraged to take part in sport in the past. It is an elite sports programme linked directly to its grass roots.

But in England we are simply not doing it. We have nothing comparable to this united approach to youth development in our national game – just 88 clubs with academies or centres of excellence ploughing their own furrow, nominally under the control of a governing body that can't even inspect their facilities let alone influence, guide or lead the quality of coaching.

It's no wonder England's national teams are lagging behind the best in the world.

CHAPTER 13

SO, WHAT'S NEXT?

So what is the future of youth development in England? A decade after the first academies and centres of excellence opened, what tangible changes have there been – and what amendments are needed in order to make things work better in the future? In short, what's next?

Only one thing is certain – opinion is divided. To some people, the future is filled with optimism and there is a golden, glowing sun just over the horizon. To others the future is painted black – English football is staring into a deep, dark abyss.

What follows is a snapshot of the broad range of arguments and ideas held by a wide variety of people in the game. Some voice their concerns and opinions in a more heartfelt way than others. Many undoubtedly represent the interests of the organisations they work for and, who ultimately pay their wages.

Let's start with the view from Soho Square. In September 2008 the FA laid out its four-year coaching strategy for 2008 to 2012. In terms of its impact on the future of youth development, the FA's plans include drawing up and rolling out a new range of age-appropriate coaching courses, training thousands of coaches at all levels (though mainly at the introductory levels), a plan to reach 1 million children via their Tesco Skills coaching programme, to stimulate development of the game via support for grass roots clubs and, of course, attempting to get the National Football Centre at Burton-upon-Trent off the ground.

Les Howie is the FA's national club development manager who has 18 grass roots regional development managers, nine supporting coach education at county FA level and nine others delivering skills coaching for 5 to 11 year olds, in charge of 90 coaches overall. Howie also oversees the FA Club Development Programme, which supports grass roots clubs, in particular their kite-marked Charter Standard clubs, and ultimately the 430,000 volunteers who, as Les puts it, 'make it happen every week'.

'There is optimism. The positive side I see is under-10s games where boys run with the ball and will do drag backs and Zidane turns,' says Howie, who played and later coached at the famous Wallsend Boys Club in Newcastle (whose alumni include Alan Shearer, Robbie Elliott, Lee Clark, Steve Bruce, Michael Carrick, Peter Beardsley, Brian Laws and Steve Watson.) 'I might not have seen that sort of thing ten years ago. Back then just 1 per cent of junior clubs had qualified coaches and that figure is now over 50 per cent.

'We now have 400 community clubs with teams from juniors right through to seniors – that's 54 per cent coverage of youth football in the country. Through the FA coaching development strategy we say we want to push that up to 75 per cent,' said Howie.

He added that Toon legend Beardsley, a player who started at Wallsend but made his way through from his local professional club, Newcastle United, to England fame, has returned to play recreationally at Wallsend as a senior on Friday afternoons.

The FA also seems to be buying into the philosophy of the Give Us Back Our Game campaign, talking about making football coaching fun for children so that they don't develop in a competitive environment that ultimately proves off-putting. 'A lot of it is about recreating the way we used to play on the streets', Howie reveals. 'I think the whole nature of society has changed – we wrap ourselves in cotton wool, don't we? It is about creating a learning environment where kids learn that it is OK to make mistakes as long as they learn from it so they will want to get it right next time.

'We have to make sure every player has the opportunity to get better and learn skills. It is not about adults turning up saying, "I'm from the FA, I've got all the badges, now let me show you how good

I am." It is about guided learning. It is about learning to run, pass, shoot and dribble – the things that excite us when we go to watch games. We have been coaching that out of them at an early age – usually because of adults wanting to win for their own gratification. That has to change and it is changing.

'There are reasons to be optimistic,' he says. 'But we are at a crossroads. We need better communications between grass roots clubs, non-League clubs and the professional game. We have to decide whether we are actually going to push ahead together to raise standards right across the game.'

So how do the leagues feel the academy system is shaping up? 'We think it has gone very well. We are proud of what has been accomplished and the way that clubs have invested in their academies,' said Premier League general secretary, Mike Foster.

'Every corner of the country is covered by an academy or a centre of excellence,' added Michael Tattersall, the Football League's deputy operations director. 'Virtually all the clubs are participating so they must feel it is beneficial otherwise they wouldn't do it. It is a success.'

Alan Sykes, chief executive of League Football Education, the charity that is delivering education programmes at Football League academies and centres of excellence, is also pleased with the progress being made. He said, 'I believe the way youth development is run in the Football League has never been stronger and I don't think either the League or the clubs are given enough credit for the work they do. If I look at where we are today, at the work we do and compare it to where we were when I started at Huddersfield 16 years ago, it is completely different.'

Yet at the time of writing this book, there is no single body controlling youth development after the collapse of the Professional Game Youth Development Group (PGYDG) in January 2009. Although the leagues insist they are pressing ahead with implementing their parts of the 2007 *Lewis Report* – how can this happen if the main bodies cannot even sit around the table together?

Nonetheless the Premier League and Football League's technical people continue with their optimistic theme. Are we producing better players than ever? 'Without question,' insists Huw Jennings, the

Premier League's former head of youth development, now academy director at Fulham. 'If you speak to most youth developers, they will tell you the skill levels, the ball mastery, balance reception and flexibility of our young players is better than it has ever been.'

Jennings says he does not look at the performance of the national team as a barometer of success – but Graham Hawkins, head of player development at the Football League, is one person who is happy to do that. 'Go and talk to every one of the national team managers and they will say our players are good enough. The view nationally is that we're rubbish and technically deficient – but the national teams are getting better and winning games. It was in a mess ten years ago but now it couldn't be better. We have seen marked improvements in player development and we now need to give the players the opportunity to progress.'

'I think we will see over the next two or three years that the players who have come through the elite system are better,' chipped in Jim Briden, the Football League's youth development business manager.

But this isn't how many of the game's more technically minded and, dare I say, more senior figures from outside the leagues view the current situation. 'I worry about the game in England,' said Brian Jones, academy director at Aston Villa. 'As far as the England national team goes, the World Cup in South Africa in 2010 will be our last real opportunity, in my opinion, to have a go at winning it, because I can't see enough quality coming through the system at youth level to replace the current side.'

The PFA's *Meltdown* report, produced in 2007, roundly hammered the lack of opportunities being handed out to home-grown players and the increasing number of foreign players now occupying places in Premier League starting line-ups – warning that England fans had better get used to seeing their team failing to reach the final stages of major competitions. 'England's failure to qualify for the Euro 2008 finals has many causes but only one source – English football is running out of English players,' the report concluded.

The report's evidence makes grim reading. 'In the 2006-07 season, 498 players started Premier League games. Of these, only 191 were English – just 38 per cent … [This] was no fluke. The number of

English players starting Premier League matches has fallen in 11 of the 15 seasons since the Premier League began and in the four seasons when English numbers increased, the increase was statistically insignificant... We are down to the bare bones. By comparison with 1992-93, the season the Premier League began, the percentage of English players starting matches in the top flight has shrunk by 47 per cent,' the report stated.

Howard Wilkinson, the man who devised the academy system in the FA's *Charter for Quality* in 1997 and who was brought back as an independent chairman of the ultimately unsuccessful PGYDG in 2008, agrees with this gloomy forecast. 'I am starting to lose hope,' he confessed. 'Some people are using smoke and mirrors to claim it is all working OK and that everything in the garden is beautiful. There are some fantastic youth developers and there is some fantastic work being done – you have to mention that – but it needs structural change. Somewhere our 18 year olds need to get a better chance to play competitive football so they can develop.

'You don't need to be a wise old football man to notice this – you just need to do your maths. Look at the research for successful international teams in European Championships and World Cups. Their players are competing for the top five teams in the top five leagues in Europe and if you look at the numbers of French, Brazilian, Italian and Spanish players, they've got more than us. Our numbers are going down – theirs are going up. You don't have to be a genius to work it out.'

Huw Jennings at Fulham shares Wilkinson's concerns about older players in the youth development system. However, Jennings blames the football authorities rather than the clubs. 'There is huge frustration that we lack direction at all levels – among the Leagues, the FA, the League Managers Association and others – and that we cannot come up with a structure that helps players in that final part of youth development – the 17 to 21 year olds,' he said.

'From where I am sitting, there is not enough understanding that we must provide a structure for those young players to succeed. We get players to 17 and then all of a sudden they go into a wilderness. If you look at the ages when players make their debuts across Europe the average age is 20, 21, and 22 – the average age for an English youngster to make his debut is 18 years and 4 months. Those players aren't ready. They may get in for a few games, but they're not ready long term. Often they are consigned to the scrapheap because people think they're not good enough.'

To help stimulate opportunity for home-grown players, the Football League introduced a quota system at the start of the 2009-10 season, although this only insists that its member clubs must field four home-grown players in their 16-man starting line-ups – a modest target.

Sir Trevor Brooking, the FA development director, has expressed long-held concerns about the quality of 5- to 11-year-old players. His somewhat contentious opinion, which has put him at odds with the Leagues, is that the clubs should go back to concentrating on developing players between the ages of 12 and 21 and leave the FA to develop younger players in an environment that isn't based on competition or the pressure or status of signing to a professional club.

'We feel that kids below the age of 12 should work with coaches outside the club structure,' says Brooking. 'From the clubs point of view, if they appoint a full-time coach to work with under-9s and under-10s they won't see the benefit in their first team of that appointment for another nine or ten years. So what you often have are the least experienced, least qualified coaches working with these age groups. At the older age groups you have the best coaches, but they are working with damaged goods, because they haven't got the appropriate skills.'

'My point is there aren't enough good young players who are elite standard. At the youngest ages, from 5 to 11, we've got to make it fun again. We have to find the fun philosophy – so each player gets a ball to play with and it isn't about assessment and results.

'The only way you can improve at football is to have contact time with the ball. The biggest problem we have to address is getting a broad base of players. In my day any technique you needed was there when you left primary school.

'We're looking at the 11 to 16 age group now – but are finding that the coaching in that age group is obsessed with competitiveness, even at grass roots level, so unless we get all the 5 to 11 stuff sorted and then follow it through then it just won't work.

'Most clubs have someone allocated to the youth development role at executive level. Some understand it, some don't. Some will see the under-12s losing three games in a row as failure and will want to scrap the whole team. Some coaches hope no one at senior level takes an interest because they don't really understand that losing six games in a row doesn't matter as long as the one person coming through the group is progressing.'

Sir Trevor's view is not widely shared by the clubs – whose need to find and register the best players has seen them driving down the age at which boys are recruited. As we have already seen this is now common at nine and can go down to as young as four years old.

However, most people do agree that the quality of coaching has improved. 'I think we are as good as anyone in Europe now – I really do,' said Dave Parnaby at Middlesbrough. 'The coaching and the environment are better in this country than ever. I would challenge anyone to say that Mark Proctor, who is coaching at 16- to 18-year-old level at my club, Middlesbrough, or someone like Paul McGuinness at Manchester United, are not as good as anyone in Europe.'

Although academies were introduced as a means of reducing the number of games boys were playing – a move that has already proved successful – some people, including Richard Lewis in his 2007 report, would like to see younger boys playing in local festivals and mini-tournaments to replace the long journeys up and down the country necessary to fulfil league fixtures. This wastes valuable time that boys could spend working on their skills.

'One of the problems across the whole of football is the number of matches that are played and it gets in the way of development,' said sports scientist, Rick Fenoglio. 'We are living in a results-driven society so that even at ages 12 to 14 people look at the results and make judgements about the coach and his professional future.

'Too much competition is bad for development. If you want to improve a young boy at football you have to spend time on tactics, set plays, teamwork and team building.

'I'm not saying playing matches is bad but it does get in the way if you are trying to optimise the child's development. Doing fitness and physiology is fine – but it is taking them away from technique, which is the most important thing.'

Many academy directors are in favour of coaching boys from a later age – usually 12 years old, after they have started at secondary school. Some are prepared to say so publicly – most are not. Brian Jones is one of those who would prefer under-12 year olds just to come to Aston Villa for weekend coaching.

Jones bemoans the lack of schools football – and points the finger not at the football industry but at government and the education system, 'When I first came to Birmingham there were 46 schools in Aston and every single one of them participated in the school leagues on a Saturday. How can we input into schools to replicate what went on 30 years ago? It takes government and money, simple as that, and until the government decides to pay PE teachers a decent salary to do after-school coaching you can forget grass roots football.'

The view of the Football League is that whatever is being said they are producing senior players – some 600 between 2004 and 2008, (which sounds impressive, although breaking it down it only works out at two players per club per season). Graham Hawkins believes the advances should not go unrecognised, 'We try to drive standards up. We pass on information and share good practice. There are many clubs with their own innovations, who are willing to share them, enabling the Football League to pass them on to other clubs. There are so many initiatives that have been integrated into the system you wouldn't recognise what goes on now compared to 11 years ago. We now have qualified physiotherapists, sports scientists, video technicians, sports psychologists, education officers and welfare officers. We are putting a lot of Continuous Personal Development (CPD) programmes together in an attempt to cover all these positions, now seen as essential in the development of the elite football player.'

The biggest change on the horizon for youth development is accountability – with the publication of education results and Ofsted-style inspection reports that parents and other interested parties can access. 'I think we all realise the need for an independent standards unit,' said Mike Foster. 'If we can get that off the ground and look to harmonise the rules, it will demonstrate that we can get results.' Michael Tattersall added, 'We haven't given up on the idea of an independent standards unit, a football version of Ofsted if you like, and we have come up with further proposals for an independent standards unit to assess clubs in the Football and Premier League.'

In terms of regular education results for 16- to 18-year-old apprentices, the figures, according to Alan Sykes of League Football Education, are already there. 'What we are starting to see are Football League clubs using education as a marketing tool to get young players into their club. So when they are talking to parents they are saying "this is what we are doing in terms of education with our apprentices".

'Last year we produced a performance report for every club. We benchmarked every club against what LFE had produced nationally and broke it down in terms of academic performance, retention and ethnicity within the academy or centre of excellence. We showed them how many apprentices they had taken on, how many had signed professional contracts and we gave it to every single club. What we haven't done, in contrast, to mainstream education, is published that information. But the clubs know where they stand in comparison to the national average. We send copies to each club chairman, chief executive and the youth development staff – so there is no hiding place. Making them public is something we may do in the future, but this was a massive culture shock to the past.'

There are also concerns about how representative club academies are of the entire football playing community. Butch Fazal, chairman of Asians in Football, has his doubts. He is calling for detailed research to be conducted into the ethnic make-up of boys playing in the country's football academies and centres of excellence. 'It is very difficult to ascertain how many Black and Minority Ethnic (BME) boys are playing in academies and centres of excellence, because filling in ethnicity forms is not mandatory so we cannot get accurate data,' said Fazal, who also runs Luton United – the biggest BME youth organisation in Bedfordshire – a club that runs nine teams for between 180 and 200 players, but has never had a single player signed to a professional club academy or centre of excellence.

Fazal is concerned about the lack of investment in the sport at the grass roots level and the poor standards of facilities due to local council cutbacks around the country. He also claims that too many football scouts do not understand the BME community, 'they do not relate or connect to the black and ethnic minority community. Football is our national sport – we need to see an end to inequality and the opening up of opportunities. If that means some players need assistance, support and guidance, it should be provided.'

Fazal is particularly worried that academy places are being given to players whose parents can guarantee getting them to the training centres which are located in the countryside. 'The 4x4 generation of players has to change. Ethnic minorities have to battle their economic disadvantage and race in order to progress in academies. A lot of BME parents probably don't help because they are wary of their own experiences in sport. Lots of seven and eight year olds – the age when boys are getting into academies – are being held back and don't aspire to it."

That may seem like a political point to make – but, sadly, many people feel the wrangling for control of the academy system has become such an intense quasi-political battle that these sort of social concerns, plus the education and welfare issues that have been addressed in this book, have been put to one side as the war continues to rage.

'Unfortunately, with the politics in the game it's a shambles really,' says Dave Parnaby at Middlesbrough. 'I think politics have slowed the development down and there's a lack of sensible and honest communication.

'The three main governing bodies don't seem to be able to converse, let alone discuss and make decisions. We are in favour of a national youth development programme at this club. We believe that our governing body should be making all the decisions regarding youth development as far as a national programme is concerned. There should be one set of rules laid down by the FA and administered by the Premier League and Football League. It would make things a lot easier.

'The FA should appoint technically minded people who understand coaching and child development to make informed decisions about the next stage of the *Charter for Quality*, because I think it has done well and I would defy anyone to say it hasn't.'

The view of Culture, Media and Sport Minister Andy Burnham is rather more positive. He acknowledged some of the problems in football youth development, but insists that the game needs to shift the focus back to the welfare of the players moving through the system. 'It is not a complete negative,' said Burnham. 'There are some marvellous social structures around football. My brother manages the team that my nephew and son play for and I usually end up putting the nets up every Saturday. Football has a great social structure and its talent identification comes from that.

'I would make a general appeal for more accountability, more independence and more rigour in how we assess what academies are doing, and for the need to provide more key statistics for parents, not just about football but about personal and social development. Football has to manage its expectations all the way through. Everyone would do well to pause for thought to consider what that does to a young person. We must do that better.'

However, others believe that youth development is immersed in the power shift that has taken place in the English game over the past 15 years. 'The FA is powerless. The power broker in the game in this country is now the Premier League,' insists Dave Woollaston of the English Schools FA. 'Professional sport is driven by money and the Premier League makes more money than the FA and all the rest put together. In fact, the Premier League is actually feeding the rest of the game.'

And there's the rub. While Premier League clubs could probably afford to build several Burtons between them, the FA don't have that luxury – they have to be more circumspect with their cash. The fact is that the FA no longer has control over the academy system it devised, and therefore no control over England's footballing future.

CONCLUSION

BACK TO THE FUTURE .

At the start of this book, I made my views clear. I believe in putting the child's interests first – as did Howard Wilkinson in *A Charter for Quality* in 1997 and Richard Lewis in *A Review of Young Player Development in Professional Football* in 2007.

In fact, everyone concerned agrees with this view but frankly some are paid to say so. While I am not jaundiced enough necessarily to share the view of one interviewee who said that the interests of children are 'a f****** million miles away from their [professional football clubs] thinking,' I understand where he is coming from. I just think some people's reasoning gets clouded. Why else would you tell a little six-year-old boy and his mum he has been culled from their football club?

A lot of the arguments that have been voiced in this book make sense. Brian Jones's idea of halving the number of boys in academies and centres of excellence is the most obvious one that stands out. This would immediately save 5,000 boys a season from the heartbreak of being released. It would also save 5,000 sets of parents from having to ship their kids back and forth to academies at least three times a week – a fact that makes a compelling environmental case all on its own.

I know the counter view – that they are being offered the chance to live the dream and receive quality coaching as well as being required to ensure that there is a full team assembled at each age range – but this holds little water. There are simply not 10,000 devastatingly brilliant young footballers in England. At best there are only opportunities for a couple of hundred to be offered professional contracts each season. When they lay their cards on the table most of the people working in youth development will tell you that the majority of boys are there to make up the numbers for the handful of really talented ones who stand a chance of making it.

I have also met too many players and parents that are cut up by this. I get angry when I speak to people in the game who just dismiss these parents as pushy, and say, in effect, that they should consider themselves lucky that anyone in professional football can be bothered to coach their kids in the first place. None of the parents featured in this book strike me as matching that particular stereotype. It is equally disingenuous to suggest that youngsters should pay to be trained. After all, aren't football clubs seeking to profit from these players?

I have been asked by the Premier and Football Leagues to pass over the details of the cases mentioned in this book so that they can investigate any claims I make. I am unwilling to do so. That would miss the point. I am not out to name and shame the clubs, as I don't really know how good or bad they are in the hierarchy of academies and centres of excellence. I have only mentioned the Walls and the Craigs in Birmingham because I came across their stories through my work as a journalist and their stories were reported on BBC Radio 5 Live. If the game took its research seriously it would unearth these experiences anyway. The fact that it doesn't leads me to think that not enough people working in football youth development care about their customers.

To those that make excuses for the horrible stories relayed in this book, I would ask the following questions: Would you want your son to receive a 'Dear John' letter from a football club on his birthday? Would you want your son to be released from a football club centre of excellence two weeks after seeing you dragged out of your car, pummelled, robbed, kicked in the head and spitting blood? Would you want your son to be told he has been 'culled'?

The system will only get better when the people doing this kind of thing are weeded out. If they feared sanction for their bad practice, would they even dream of doing it in the first place? If they were paid more than £25 a session, would they adopt better practice?

My take – like so many others – is let's head back to the future.

Give Us Back Our Game offer a refreshingly simple view. Leave it to the kids to decide the rules. Watch any group of children playing and you will see that they make it work for themselves. Play works. Endless academic study highlights this. It is why huge sums of money are being invested by government in play and playground design. To play sport children just need guidance. What kids need in football are plenty of touches of the ball and the chance to experiment. That is why Manchester United's Under-10s programme is to be applauded. It is based on simple but effective principles.

The FA's idea of letting players develop regionally until they reach secondary school also makes sense. The reason clubs are looking to teach kids in nappies – culling six year olds, trawling and trading and doing whatever else they deem fit and fair – is because they want to sign the best players as young as possible. To the clubs they are commodities, not kids. This is an unavoidable fact. Unfortunately, the FA caused this to happen by designing a system, set out in *A Charter for Quality* in 1997, that was intended, but didn't grasp the selfishness of clubs. It is ridiculous it has taken the FA 12 years to come up with the age-appropriate coaching courses that should have been available when the academies and centres of excellence first opened. The FA revealed even more confused thinking when it mothballed the National Football Centre at Burton-upon-Trent in preference to re-building Wembley and taking on a huge debt. No wonder the Leagues are at the end of their tether.

There is, of course, absolutely no excuse for the ridiculous political differences between the various bodies running our national game. Perhaps this is best represented by a quick look at the north London stadium landscape. We have Wembley, the new Olympic Stadium on the way and Arsenal's Emirates Stadium – but no development centre for the national sport. It's crazy. It could be built at a fraction of the cost, but I guess football development will just have to wait. Again.

At the same time, I see the likes of Give Us Back Our Game going without funding to extend their wonderful programme. The Midland Junior Premier Football League doesn't get a penny for offering 2,500 kids – including maybe one third who've been jettisoned by professional clubs – a chance to play a decent standard of football. These lads include Ryan Craig and Nathan Wall, previously depressed boys who are now enjoying their football again. If just one Football League club grant of £180,000 were doled to that league, even more players would benefit. Perish the thought that grant aid could be rolled out nationally, to pay for administration or even coaches, to benefit thousands of young players instead of propping up a single club centre of excellence that is trying to develop, at best, 150 players for its own use.

This book has looked in some detail at the way English football academies are developing home-grown talent. Although it is hardly news that football is a ruthless business, the fact that clubs are scouting for boys as young as four is a shocking development. A considerable number of people are questioning the way this is heading, with one even suggesting – and I am not sure they were altogether joking – that genetic engineering could reach the point of 'mating' elite male and female athletes to produce perfect footballers.

I have not focussed attention on the trafficking of African boys from their own continent to major European football clubs, because it is a subject worthy of a book in its own right. This is a massive problem and bound in a web of complicated issues, not all of them sport-related and very few, when all is said and done, purely about football. That said, with some English clubs forming links, even wholly owning clubs in continental Europe, Africa, China and closer to home – that stock-in-trade supplier of English football talent, Ireland – you have to wonder where it is heading.

The main focus of this book has been to explore the integrity of the youth development system in England. The dearth of home-grown talent means that clubs will inevitably look overseas. It isn't just for players that the English game now looks abroad – it also does so for club owners, sponsors and fans, with the Premier League mooting the idea of playing the '39th game' (the proposed international round of matches) so it can expand its global 'branding'. In short it is all about making money.

But the idea of making the essential lifeblood of English football – its domestic players and fans – redundant is a ridiculous concept. What good is having the swankiest league in the world, the best stadiums and a plethora of world class stars playing in the Premier League unless there is some tangible improvement in the performance of England national teams at world level?

You could forgive some of the education and welfare problems if it was remotely justifiable in terms of the quality and quantity of players that England's managers have had at their disposal in the last ten years. But the sad fact is there just aren't enough high-quality, home-grown players who can grace the world stage. Surely at the very minimum the spiriting of 10,000 boys through an elite academy system each year should have delivered strength in depth? How long can England preserve the illusion that it is a major football-playing country unless its national team starts to win competitions?

When Sky TV launched its coverage of the brand new Premier League back in 1992 it was under the banner 'A Whole New Ball Game'. That is what it has become – and that is what it will remain if England's top clubs refuse to develop and field English talent. If you take it one step further, why bother playing games in England at all if the fans are not rich enough or can't relate to the multinational array of players, or if the franchise doesn't quite fit anymore? Why not dump the English players completely? After all Chelsea, Arsenal, Man Utd and Liverpool are just names; they are no different from Vodafone, Siemens, Nokia, Tesco, HSBC or Gillette.

I worked in China for four months in 2008 and all the people I worked with, to one degree or another, supported a top European, mainly English, football team. In conversations they could merrily move the world's best players around on football's international chess table. That is what interests them. No one cares if Steven Gerrard or Jamie Carragher are local Liverpool lads. None of the new-found faraway fans of Liverpool or Man Utd have heard of Hillsborough or Munich, but they could have a damn good stab at listing 40-odd players these clubs now have in their squads. It is no good rolling out the themes of passion or history – they don't mean a thing. These are just the big brands of world football.

So what chance does youth development in English football stand in this context? As a society, England is struggling to keep its kids active – let alone hope they can become good footballers. They have the same problems as most other youngsters who are fixated with PCs, mobile phones and games consoles and spend most of their time staring at screens. They do not play outside for fear of being run over, preyed upon by paedophiles, drug pushers or hoodie-wearing gangs. Mainly these are the fears of parents. Understandable fears, but surely part of a national moral panic?

Kids get blamed for eating fatty foods, drinking alcopops and sugary beverages, and are endlessly harangued for a range of anti-social behaviours. And when they retreat to that time-honoured escape route of playing footy, there are adults trying to organise them, select them, coach them, cheat on their behalf to help them win and behaving appallingly (if you think I'm joking then go and visit your average county FA office on a Monday when the weekend's disciplinary reports come in). And then there are scouts from professional clubs on the side looking to wheel them away with the promise of a better life.

Dave Woollaston, an English Schools' FA coach and careers teacher, is much quoted in this book. He told me that he used to get children sitting in front of him who wanted to be doctors, nurses, to drive trains or planes or be pop stars and footballers. Now, in a world of talent shows and reality TV, they just want to be 'famous'. They don't know what they want to be famous for doing or what the best way is of getting there (sitting in a mock house with TV cameras trained on them for 14 weeks and acting up a bit seems as easy as any option), or what it will be like to be famous. They just want to *be* famous. They don't want to earn it – they just want to be it.

Small wonder an England player at the 2002 World Cup was allegedly overheard describing the prospect of gathering a winner's medal as a being a great potential 'fanny magnet'. How about winning the games first, pal?

You look at the onward march of foreign players into the top leagues and wonder where it will end. When boys being shipped in from Europe, Africa and South America and elsewhere at 16, spend three years here and are classified as home-grown. It's not the British game's fault; it's UEFA's somewhat strange definition, but it renders 'home-grown' statistics meaningless.

Despite everything, English football is powered by incredible passion. There really isn't anything to rival it for intense culture. As fans, we believe and we want to believe. We hope our clubs will produce the next Busby Babes or Class of '92 – we love it when one of our own (who seemingly 'wants it more') is plucked from the local community and becomes a folklore hero. It is just so incredibly rare these days. Football is important to us and we want youth development to work – we want it to make sense.

The interviews for this book over the years have been draining – I don't want to moan, for there is much to be happy about in football – but meeting distraught parents, angry coaches and dismayed administrators has had its effects. I have met coaches who, off the record, have told me all kinds of things they feel they cannot mention to directors at their clubs, either because they won't get a sympathetic hearing or fear that if they speak out they may risk getting the sack – yet they are delivering a programme of excellence they don't have confidence in. Why do they speak to me? Because they just want to tell someone who will listen.

As we head into recession, will the bubble we were promised would never burst – the Premier League and all its upwardly mobile momentum – go into reverse? How recession proof are all those satellite TV subscriptions, the £50 tickets, the £40 replica shirts and other paraphernalia? How sexy will soccer seem when it's on the slide – when the top foreigners look to earn a fast buck elsewhere? Then, maybe, the game will have to turn to its youth – but will they be good enough to spark the revolution? We'd better hope so.